THE ULTIMATE GUIDE TO BUILDING A HEALTHY AND FULFILLING MARRIAGE

STRATEGIES FOR FORGIVENESS, LOVE, AND GRACE

W. AUSTIN GARDNER

W. AUSTIN GARDNER

The Ultimate Guide to Building a Healthy and Fulfilling Marriage

Strategies for Forgiveness, Love, and Grace

∽

∽

Thank you for finding your marriage to be so important that you will take the time to work together for a happy and fulfilling relationship.

ABOUT THE AUTHOR

Here to Save Your Marriage!

Dear husbands and wives,

I understand your challenges in rebuilding trust and restoring intimacy in your marriage. I've been there many times with many couples and am here to help you.

I wrote 'The Ultimate Guide to Building a Healthy and Fulfilling Marriage' because I have seen firsthand the power of forgiveness, love, and grace in a marriage. This book is a comprehensive guide that covers key strategies and principles for building a strong and fulfilling marriage. After over 50 years of marriage and a career as a pastor, missionary, counselor, and marriage conference speaker, I have witnessed countless marriages survive and thrive by implementing these strategies.

As someone who got married at 18, has a beautiful marriage of over 50 years, and has since preached hundreds of marriage conferences and counseled many struggling couples, I am uniquely qualified to help you reach your goals of a happy and fulfilling marriage. I have also performed the weddings of all four of my children and have three happily married grandchildren, proving that the principles I teach in this book are practical and personally important to me.

So, you're ready to take the first step towards rebuilding trust and restoring intimacy in your marriage. In that case, I urge you to start reading "The Ultimate Guide to Building a Healthy and Fulfilling Marriage" right now. Let my years of experience as a coach, marriage counselor, and mentor guide you toward a stronger, more loving relationship with your partner.

I believe in you, and I believe in the power of a healthy and fulfilling marriage. Let's start this journey together.

With love,
    W. Austin Gardner

The best way to rebuild a healthy and fulfilling marriage is to start by rebuilding the trust and connection with your partner. It takes time, effort, and commitment, but the reward of a strong and loving relationship is well worth it.

Dedicated to my extremely loved wife Betty, my partner, confidante, and rock. Through over 50 years of marriage, we have weathered countless storms, celebrated endless joys, and faced life's challenges side by side. Your unwavering love, grace, and strength have inspired and supported me. This book is a testament to the enduring power of our love and the wisdom we've gained on our journey together. Here's to many more years of love, laughter, and adventure. I love you always and forever.

Austin

ACKNOWLEDGMENTS

I want to express my deepest gratitude to my wife, Betty. Your unwavering love, support, and strength have been the foundation of our family and the inspiration behind this book. I am particularly grateful for the way you stood by me during over twelve years of cancer, nearly dying from COVID-19, extensive surgeries, and all the struggles and chaos of life, showing your resilience and grace in the face of life's challenges. Your presence in my life is a constant source of strength, and I am forever grateful to you.

I also want to acknowledge our beautiful family - our four children, their spouses, our beloved grandchildren, and great-grandchildren. Your love, encouragement, and unwavering faith have inspired me countless times. Your role in living out the principles of forgiveness, love, and grace that I have preached and taught has given me first-hand insight and has been invaluable in shaping the message of this book.

I owe all of you a debt of gratitude that I can never fully repay. Your love and support have been the driving force behind my work, and I am blessed to have each of you in my life. Thank you for embodying the ideas and values I cherish so deeply.

Finally, I want to acknowledge God's immeasurable grace and blessings. Without Him, none of this would have been possible. His guidance and love have sustained us through every trial and triumph, and for that, I am eternally grateful. I am humbled by His love and faithfulness, and I feel truly blessed to have experienced His presence in our lives.

My heartfelt appreciation

Austin

INTRODUCTION

The Golden Wedding Anniversary marks a remarkable milestone in the contemporary era. Betty and I joyously commemorated our 50th year of marriage on August 18, 2023, surrounded by our cherished four children and their families. Through the decades, we witnessed the growth of our four children from tender ages to adulthood, witnessing their weddings and the arrival of grandchildren. Today, our family has expanded to include our beloved four children and their spouses, twenty adored grand-children with their spouses, and a delightful great-granddaughter, creating a legacy of love and togetherness that spans generations. We now make a total of thirty five.

GOD'S GRACE has genuinely blessed Betty and me. From falling in love to the sacred union of marriage, we have journeyed through every stage with gratitude. Witnessing our children's weddings and seeing our grandchildren embark on their journeys of love and matrimony fills us with immense joy and a deep sense of fulfillment.

· · ·

GOD HAS GUIDED OUR LIVES, shaping our journey through various experiences, including moments of hardship we faced together. Despite times when the challenges seemed insurmountable, God's presence and providence always saw us through. In every circumstance, even amidst what appeared to be disasters, we've witnessed God's transformative power, turning trials into unexpected blessings for us as His beloved children.

BETTY and I never dreamed of all God had in store for us. God allowed us to see great things in our ministry, from starting churches and training leaders to seeing thousands of people come to Jesus as their personal Lord and Savior.

WE'VE ALSO ENDURED profound heartache. Individuals we trusted and believed loved us mistreated our children, and we witnessed it. We stood vigil by their beds as they suffered through broken bones, high fevers, diabetes, typhoid, hepatitis, and many other challenges.

I HAVE DEALT with several health issues. Starting with losing a kidney to cancer in June 2012, then being on a ventilator for 21 days with COVID-19 in June 2020, and then being placed in palliative care. I suffered from extreme diarrhea because of the cancer medicines until a surgeon said he believed he might get all the cancer. I lost my adrenal glands and right testicle to my returning cancer in September 2022. My surgeon says there is a 50% chance my cancer will return. The loss of my adrenal glands brought more excitement to our lives. The doctor says that if I miss two days of medication, my steroids I die. Adrenal glands are central to most everything in our lives.

. . .

OUR FAMILY HAS WEATHERED many storms, yet our marriage has consistently been the cornerstone of my existence. Even now, our love remains profound, and we are both excited about the journey we continue to share.

OVER THE PAST 50 YEARS, I've dedicated myself to serving as a pastor, missionary, and leader trainer, investing countless hours in conversations with young couples. I've had the privilege of officiating dozens of weddings, offering guidance and counseling to these couples before and after their marriage ceremonies.

Only six marriages in a hundred are truly fulfilling.   *Howard Hendricks*[1]

WE ALL DREAM of a healthy and fulfilling marriage, but few know how to realize that a beautiful relationship is yours for the taking. If you will, simply learn from your relationship with God and apply that to your marriage and family.

THERE ARE TIMES WE FEEL WE'D DO ANYTHING TO HAVE IT.

WE'VE WITNESSED marriages in their most challenging moments, grappling with issues like spousal betrayal, rape, homosexuality, pornography, and various emotional struggles. Despite these daunting circumstances, we've had the opportunity to witness how

God's grace, Word, and Holy Spirit can profoundly transform lives and bring redemption and healing.

LET me guide you through constructing or revitalizing a joyful, thriving marriage within these pages. Your marital bond surpasses any other relationship in importance. While I don't possess all the answers, I know the One who does.

THE HOLY SPIRIT has graciously provided us with divine plans and blueprints for crafting the marriage we envision, all within the pages of your Bible. By submitting to the Holy Spirit and staying sensitive to His guidance and instructions, God has the power and willingness to rescue and restore your marriage.

I'VE WITNESSED marriages lifted out of despair and transformed by the timeless wisdom found in the Bible. The efficacy and accuracy of God's Word have been demonstrated repeatedly in the lives of countless individuals! I firmly believe that the Bible provides solutions for every situation we encounter. It's not merely an antiquated book that sits decoratively on a coffee table; it's a dynamic instruction manual that pertains to every facet of our earthly existence: our work, our relationships, our children, and primarily our marriages.

GOD HAS GRACIOUSLY PROVIDED us with a comprehensive guidebook that answers life's trials and tribulations. Seeing how often we dismiss it as an outdated rulebook is discouraging! Consequently, the church has become a source of contention, a burden many bear to uphold social standing or avoid disappointing elderly relatives. People's trust in the Bible and the church appears to be dwindling as they struggle to find relevance between its teachings and everyday challenges.

. . .

DON'T FALL FOR THE LIE THAT YOU WEREN'T MEANT TO HAVE A HAPPY HOME!

GOD IS A GOD OF RELATIONSHIPS. The Father, Son, and Holy Spirit coexist in a perfect and harmonious relationship. God loves you and seeks you to restore you to your relationship with Him. So, the Bible isn't about rules. It is about relationships. Therefore, no one knows more about helping us build a relationship than God does. God is love. The teaching of God is to love. God loves through us.

WHEN WE DISMISS the Bible and it's truth there comes a loss of belief in the purpose of our lives and a weakening of our faith in a good God. However, we must settle something within our hearts before we delve into solutions. The Bible is unequivocal - healthy and happy marriages are attainable! A "healthy, happy marriage" is not an archaic concept relegated to a bygone era; instead, it remains the cornerstone of our society and blessings in this current generation. Do not let yourself be deceived into thinking that a joyful marriage and fulfilling home life are out of reach! While statistics may paint a bleak picture, they only tell part of the story, and it's important not to let them define our beliefs or aspirations.

IF I WERE to rely solely on experts' predictions, my marriage should have ended long ago! According to statistics, we're all destined for failure, with little hope for our marriages to thrive.

. . .

THANKFULLY, we serve a God who defies statistics! Throughout my years in ministry, I've witnessed families overcome seemingly insurmountable challenges and heal from deep brokenness. I've seen miracles unfold within the very walls of people's homes, surpassing anything I've witnessed elsewhere. God desires to bring the same restoration and transformation to your life and your family!

FOR YEARS, my passion has centered on preaching, teaching, and writing about the importance of marriage and the home:

1. It has been a source of immeasurable joy and security.
2. Its significance in shaping our society and the world is unparalleled and irreplaceable.
3. Indeed, not least, the profound symbolism of marriage represents Jesus Christ's love for us, painting a beautiful portrait of His eternal care and devotion.

IN THIS BOOK, I urge you to adopt this perspective. Despite the thousands of professors and politicians who dismiss the significance of marriage in our society, the picture of Christ's love remains a powerful truth that motivates us to pursue a better marriage, even during challenging times. Jesus' love for the church is an anchor when we feel like giving up, encouraging us to persevere and hold on.

THERE IS a key verse that I believe God intends for us to use as a cornerstone for building healthy and fulfilling marriages. It summarizes all that we hope to accomplish in our families.

Husbands, love your wives, even as Christ also loved the church, and gave himself for it; Ephesians 5:25.

YOU MAY HAVE READ this passage many times, skimming over its profound truth as I did for many years. We often nod in agreement, thinking, "Yes, I understand. Jesus loves the church, and we should love our spouses." Then we swiftly move on. However, it's crucial to pause and grasp the magnitude of this command. Paul is challenging us to love as the Son of God loved. So, how did He love? Uncovering this answer holds the key to establishing robust and gratifying marriages.

IN THE UPCOMING CHAPTERS, we will study Christ's love—examining how He loved us—and we'll pose reflective questions about our expressions of love toward one another in our marriage. Throughout this journey, we'll uncover six crucial principles essential for cultivating a joyful and rewarding marriage, ultimately leading us to a deeper comprehension of what it truly means to love as Christ loved.

THESE INSIGHTS WILL BE a profound exploration, especially for those facing challenges and difficulties in their marriages. You will discover an amazing, practical, and genuine solution—a practical action plan. It's common for us to express a desire for a happy and fulfilling marriage, yet we often lack clarity on how to achieve it. By learning to practice the love of Jesus toward the church, we'll reshape our perceptions of what love entails and how it functions.

AS MANY DO, you might already enjoy a healthy and fulfilling marriage. If you're fortunate to have a good marriage, you'll undoubtedly want to maintain its quality. Family life can often resemble a roller coaster ride at a theme park, with exhilarating highs and stomach-dropping lows. It can feel shaky, unpredictable, and fast-paced. You've probably heard the saying, "Time flies when you're having fun." However, I've realized that time moves swiftly regardless of whether we enjoy ourselves or face challenges. What's crucial is that we remain prepared for whatever life brings our way. We must expect moments in our marriages and while raising children that may not be as smooth as today. This book will address various issues to equip marriages for the inevitable challenges.

LIKE ANYTHING SIGNIFICANT, building a healthy and fulfilling marriage will require more time than you'd prefer, come at a higher cost than expected, and inevitably involve some mistakes. However, make a firm commitment in your heart right now to dedicate yourself to creating or recreating your healthy and fulfilling marriage. It will require effort, but it's undoubtedly better than enduring dissatisfaction in a horrible marriage, emotional divorce or actual divorce. Decide today - it's time to build!

---

1. Mark Water, *The New Encyclopedia of Christian Quotations* (Alresford, Hampshire: John Hunt Publishers Ltd, 2000), 659

1

TRUE FORGIVENESS

Throughout the years, I've witnessed the God of Heaven heal individuals, restore broken families, and mend fractured marriages. Time after time, the Bible has proven to be the source of solutions for their various needs.

AFTER SPENDING several years in ministry in Peru, some families from our church approached me with curiosity, asking, "How did you come to understand us so well? You understand our challenges, culture, and family dynamics."

THE ANSWER IS that people are people, and the Word of God knows us all too well. When I preached the Bible, it hit home. They understood that God understood them. That wasn't my wisdom but the Word of God moving in power in our lives.

REGARDLESS OF NATIONALITY, language, or race, people benefit from the Bible's wisdom and guidance. It alone can rescue us from the troubles we often encounter, including the complex challenges confronting our marriages.

Successful Marriages Imitate What Christ Did For Us!

ONCE AGAIN, the cornerstone verse upon which we will build our healthy and fulfilling marriage is the truth presented to us in...

Husbands, love your wives, even **as Christ also loved the church, and gave himself for it;** Ephesians 5:25:

LOVING as Christ loved is the essence of successful marriages—the husband's love is to mirror Christ's sacrificial love for us. That also applies to the wife.

SACRIFICIAL LOVE LEADS us to the first key for building a healthy and fulfilling marriage. Drawing from years of counseling couples and over fifty years of marriage experiences, I've realized that embodying Christlike love in this first aspect can be one of the most challenging yet crucial.

It is not what happens to you but how you respond or react.

As you cultivate a healthy and fulfilling marriage over the years, expect setbacks and disappointments. Regardless of the distance traveled on life's journey with your family, you're not immune to challenges stemming from adversarial forces. Thus, success at home isn't about your circumstances; it's about how you respond. Everyone encounters struggles; what distinguishes us is our reaction to them.

No marriage thrives because the partners are perfect or flawless, and children do not grow up well-adjusted because their parents never make mistakes. Indeed, every family faces challenges, but the key differentiator is how they respond to them.

The ideal response to the wrongs we endure from loved ones is to imitate Christ's love. Consider His reaction to the greatest betrayal: after enduring brutal flogging, humiliation, and dying a torturous death on the cross, He looked toward Heaven and declared,

> ...**Father, forgive them, for they know not what they do.** And they parted his raiment, and cast lots. Luke 23:34

Despite the profound injustice He suffered, Christ chose forgiveness. This **act of unconditional forgiveness** is what Paul urges us to imitate in our own lives, saying:

> Forbearing one another, and forgiving one another, if any man have a quarrel against any: **even as Christ forgave you, so also *do* ye.** Colossians 3:13

A MISUNDERSTANDING of forgiveness can devastate a marriage because it threatens to dismantle all that has been built. This misconception can stifle your family's healing capacity, deepening wounds and prolonging recovery. It has led to the downfall of countless marriages and families. Amidst the inevitable conflicts and disagreements, the critical question is whether we can forgive or if our grievances, our wounds, will drain the life of our relationships.

The Forgiven Forgive

FOR THOSE WHO follow Christ and have felt the profound grace of God's forgiveness, it's vital to embrace this foundational principle: those who are forgiven forgive. Just as we are called to love in the way Christ loved, we are also called to forgive as He forgives. Thus, genuine forgiveness outweighs every transgression in a healthy and fulfilling marriage, creating an environment where healing and love flourish.

What Forgiveness Means

Forgiveness is the act of

- excusing a fault or offense;
- it means to pardon,
- to let go of anger or resentment, or
- to absolve someone from a debt obligation, for instance.

LIVING IN ANY HUMAN COMMUNITY, it doesn't take long to encounter situations that call for forgiveness. Eventually, everyone makes a mistake, regardless of how long they've done the right thing.

I MET my wife in November 1972 during our college years. I was an unusual sight: a 6'1", 145-pound Tennessee redneck, and she, a refined Georgian socialite, exuding charm in moccasins and bell-bottom britches. Our first encounter happened as I was deep into fixing a car engine, embodying every bit of the hillbilly stereotype with my no-shirt, cowboy boots, and arms covered in grease. Amidst my rush to clean up, I caught sight of her and was instantly captivated. My mind raced with strategies to meet her, resolved to pursue her at every chance, and I was determined to start dating her.

I SAW Betty again on a date with one of my friends. She was so quiet, so pretty, and had the sweetest smile. I loved her then and love her now.

WHEN I INVITED her on our first date, it was for a double date, and she only went with me because she liked the "other guy!" I am chasing her here, and she has no interest, but I insisted.

WHEN I MUSTERED the courage to tell Betty I loved her, her response was a disappointing: "I love you, too... just like a brother." That was a crushing blow, far from the reaction I had hoped for. I did not intend to gain a sister; I was aiming for something much more - I wanted her to be my wife.

REMARKABLY, Betty and I glided through our dating phase without a single argument, basking in an idyllic relationship. Not once did we face a disagreement, maintaining a peaceful harmony to the altar. This streak of tranquility extended months into our marriage, devoid of quarrels. However, this romantic bubble eventually burst. Following that first clash, disagreements became a part of our journey together. Jokingly, it's always the man's fault, right?

YET, conflicts are a natural part of any lasting human connection. Avoiding them isn't the goal; learning to navigate them with grace is crucial. Recognizing that anger and resentment are inevitable, the key to enduring these challenges lies in forgiveness. To truly grasp the essence of forgiveness, let's explore its manifestations through the actions of the ultimate exemplar of forgiveness, Jesus Christ.

True forgiveness excuses the offense, though we are the offended party.

> Forbearing one another, and forgiving one another, if any man have a quarrel against any: **even as Christ forgave you, so also** *do* **ye.** Colossians 3:13

The first characteristic of genuine forgiveness lies in its ability to transcend blame. It refrains from assigning fault, sidestepping the all-too-common game of pointing fingers.

A FAMILIAR REFRAIN echoes in the trenches of marital discord: "If only he would shape up," or the classic, "I'm holding up my end; when will she do the same?" Such sentiments underscore a conditional approach to forgiveness, contingent on the other's change.

. . .

YET, consider the example set by Jesus Christ. Despite being the party wronged—His laws transgressed, His love spurned, His sacrifice required—He initiated forgiveness. His response to betrayal and injustice was not to demand retribution or to wallow in victimhood; instead, He chose to forgive, even in the face of ongoing offense.

CONTRASTINGLY, we often hesitate to forgive when wronged by a spouse or family member. Our initial reactions may include silence, bitterness, or anger, nurturing a grudge with the potential to escalate into prolonged conflict. Meanwhile, Jesus demonstrated the pinnacle of forgiveness, offering pardon amidst His crucifixion.

TRUE FORGIVENESS IS NOT JUST about absolving someone when it's easy or when justice seems served. It's about **releasing resentment and extending grace,** even under the weight of injustice—imitating a love that forgives without conditions.

True forgiveness separates the offense from the offender.

> **As far as the East is from the West,** so far hath he removed our transgressions from us. Psalms 103:12

This verse illuminates a profound truth about forgiveness: when God forgives your sins, He separates them from you entirely. Your sin no longer identifies you; it is no longer a part of who you are.

JESUS SYMBOLICALLY REMOVED your sin as far as the East is from the West—a distance with no poles. No matter how far east you go, there's always more East. Consider the vastness: You may be in the

Eastern United States, but to someone in Russia, you're still in the West. There's even Western Europe. The point is that your sins have been relocated to the ends of the Earth.

NO MATTER how hard you may try, you can never retrieve your sins. They aren't just separated from you; they have been eradicated from your being. Despite your failures and mistakes, God ensures that your sins are permanently separated from you. Imagine experiencing such complete forgiveness within your home!

WOULD you believe that even my beloved wife has wronged me at times? And I, in return, have made countless mistakes towards her. True forgiveness demands that I look at Betty and see her separate from her sins. When I focus on her sins, I lose sight of her true essence. Conversely, when I see her for who she is, I cannot see her sins—they are distinct from her, always separate.

HAVE you ever been so consumed by anger towards someone that it becomes challenging to even look at them? That's because you're struggling to detach that person's actions from their person.

IN HIS HOLINESS, God doesn't tolerate sin, so He separates our sins from us to restore our fellowship through forgiveness. He reconciled us from our sins, not imputing or counting our trespasses against us. He has done the same thing for everyone, every where. He reconciled the world to Himself.

18 And all things *are* of God, who hath **reconciled us to himself** by Jesus Christ, and hath given to us the ministry of reconciliation; 19 To wit, that God was in Christ, **reconciling the world unto**

himself, not imputing their trespasses unto them; and hath committed unto us the word of reconciliation. II Corinthians 5:18–19

SIMILARLY, you must learn to separate the sin from the person to regain harmony and friendship in your home. Today, make a conscious decision to look at your spouse or children and affirm in your heart, "Yes, there has been wrongdoing, but I choose to forgive and not let the sin overshadow you. Separating the fault from your spouse is how we'll move forward together!"

True forgiveness doesn't remember the offense.

And their sins and iniquities **will I remember no more.** Hebrews 10:17

You've probably heard countless times before that upon entering Heaven, God will invariably bring up every misdeed, every act of rebellion against Him. It's no wonder some of us harbor apprehension about reaching that destination, the judgment! However, the truth, as the Bible articulates, is that such judgment is reserved for those who have spurned His forgiveness here on Earth – not for those who have been forgiven. When God forgives, He chooses to erase the memory, the record of our offenses.

ALLOW me to share a story about Al, a man from my ministry in Peru who once walked the path of a Communist terrorist and even served time in prison for his actions. One day, he confided in me about the deep-seated guilt that plagued him regarding his past. "When I pray,"

Al admitted, "I feel as though God sees me only as a terrorist, unworthy of His acceptance."

"But, Al," I interjected, "God doesn't see you that way."

"What do you mean?" he pressed. "The Bible describes Him as omniscient – knowing all things!"

"Yes, but in this case, He chooses not to," I clarified. "The Bible teaches us that He has deliberately decided to forget your sins. He truly doesn't recall your past as a terrorist! If you were to ask Him, 'God, do you remember all the atrocities I committed before being saved?' He would reply, 'Hmm... I don't recall that, Al. It's not something I choose to remember.'"

Not only does God separate Al from his past offenses, but He also eradicates any memory of them. God is aware of everything, and knows it all yet thankfully, He doesn't retain every detail! That's the essence of God's forgiveness – He chooses to forget the wrongs we've committed against Him. As Jeremiah states,

> I will forgive their iniquity, and **I will remember their sin no more** (Jeremiah 31:34).

If you aspire to cultivate a thriving and fulfilling marriage, it's imperative to embrace forgiveness in this manner. Let go of the grievances and extend genuine forgiveness, just as God does, by choosing to forget the wrongs committed against you.

True forgiveness erases offenses from the record.

I, *even* I, *am* he that blotteth out thy transgressions for mine own sake, And will not remember thy sins. Isaiah 43:25.

God's way of erasing our mistakes from the record is truly remarkable. In His eyes, it's as though those mistakes never occurred in the first place! Isn't this concept often foreign in our marriages? Consider a scenario where you've argued.

PERHAPS YOU'VE BEEN "FORGIVEN" for the same mistake countless times. You and your spouse reconciled and moved forward. Yet, sooner or later, another disagreement arises. Then, almost miraculously, your spouse retrieves a massive mental file, exclaiming, "It's just like you always do!" and reciting a litany of past instances – the last 900 times you did the same thing!

BOTH HUSBANDS and wives are guilty of this behavior. Sometimes, we parents are just as guilty. We maintain an extensive filing system in our minds. When our children let us down, we pull out the ledger. Suddenly, the things we supposedly forgave become ammunition against the "forgiven"!

INDEED, God's forgiveness is unparalleled. He doesn't just delete the offense from the hard drive; He doesn't back it up or store it to be used against us later. Instead, He declares, "I will not remember your sins; I will blot them out from my records." What an incredible sense of relief that brings! Knowing that He isn't amassing ammunition against us is comforting and liberating.

. . .

Let forgiven things remain forgotten things!

Now, strive to forgive as He does! Make a conscious decision to wipe away the records of past wrongs. When faced with a disagreement, resist the temptation to dwell on the past and defend yourself. Choose to let forgiven things remain forgotten!

True forgiveness doesn't mention the offense again.

> He will turn again, he will have compassion upon us; He will subdue our iniquities; And **thou wilt cast all their sins into the depths of the sea.** Micah 7:19

It's beautiful that once God forgives you, He doesn't bring it up again! However, in our human relationships, it's more common to hear, "I forgave you, but I still remember it, and I'll keep mentioning it!" Isn't it frustrating when someone constantly brings up a past mistake that was supposed to be forgiven and forgotten? Eventually, it can drive a loved one away, seeking a fresh start elsewhere.

TRUE BIBLICAL FORGIVENESS is a fresh start. It wipes our record just as the blood of Christ cleanses our slate with God. There's no hidden file box in the back closet; those past wrongs are permanently erased from the hard drive and never brought up again. This kind of forgiveness enables us to continue building a healthy and fulfilling marriage even after experiencing deep offenses.

. . .

Every day is an opportunity to start anew.

Successful relationships keep short accounts.

WHEN WE CHOOSE to maintain a running tally of every wrong committed against us, we unintentionally distance ourselves from our loved ones who have offended us. It's like an unpaid credit card balance that escalates exponentially with each month's accrued interest. If family conflicts and grievances aren't promptly resolved, they can spiral into a torrent of bitterness, much like an avalanche gaining momentum.

IN A HEALTHY AND FULFILLING MARRIAGE, a spouse must be able to move beyond the repercussions of their actions. Moving on and letting go goes against our natural inclinations. Typically, when someone wrongs us, we expect them to face the full consequences of their mistake. However, even though I deserve the punishment outlined by God's law, I pay nothing when I sin. Thankfully, the God of Heaven removes the consequences from us. Jesus sacrificed Himself to bear our punishment. He didn't die because of any wrongdoing on His part but because of our offenses.

WHEN THE BIBLE describes Jesus as the "propitiation" for the sins of the entire world, it signifies that someone must bear the consequences for these sins, and Jesus willingly stepped forward to endure the punishment in our place. Instead of allowing us to face what we deserve, He offers each of us a fresh start, regardless of how undeserving we may be.

And he is the **propitiation** (sacrifice, payment, when your sins and the sins of the whole world were placed on Jesus freeing us from the penalty of sin) **for our sins:** and not for ours only, but also for *the sins of* the whole world. 1 John 2:2.

Don't let the sun go down on your wrath.

ONE OF THE most profound pieces of marriage advice can be found in

Be ye angry, and sin not: **let not the sun go down upon your wrath:** Ephesians 4:26

THESE WORDS GUIDE HANDLING conflict within a marriage. Over the years, I've emphasized to married couples that occasional disagreements are inevitable, but the Bible offers a blueprint for engaging in a spiritual, Christian way of resolving conflicts.

Do not go to bed mad!

A KEY PRINCIPLE is not letting the sun go down on unresolved anger. It acknowledges that disagreements will arise, and expressing frustration is okay. However, the crucial point is that any conflict or discord must be resolved before bedtime. We are instructed not to harbor anger towards each other by the time the sun sets. This practice is a preventive measure from allowing minor grievances to escalate into major issues that could damage the relationship.

. . .

IT'S remarkable how many couples, upon reaching the brink of divorce, can't recall the initial reasons that led to their conflicts. What might have started as a minor difference of opinion has escalated into a full-blown conflict resembling World War III, with both parties demanding unconditional surrender.

SIMILAR CONFLICTS CAN ARISE with teenage children, who often exhibit challenging attitudes at home. A simple remark can ignite an argument, leading to anger and eventual withdrawal to their rooms. Later, they may reemerge and exacerbate the situation, triggering a cycle of arguments, anger, and retreat. Teenagers are often steadfast and persistent, prolonging these conflicts until they become significant issues between parents and children.

THE SOLUTION LIES in addressing the situation promptly and proactively. Don't wait until the conflict escalates to the point of metaphorically launching nuclear missiles back and forth. It is crucial to take immediate steps to resolve conflicts and prevent them from snowballing into major problems.

Let mercies be new every morning.

Don't settle for just a truce before going to bed! We often conclude arguments by saying, "Well, we've agreed to a ceasefire for now; tomorrow, we'll resume our Cold War."

I'VE BEEN guilty of giving Betty the cold shoulder and the whole cold back! Sometimes, my body language in bed clearly communicates that I'm upset. In the past, when I weighed 270 pounds, I could practically launch her off the bed with my movements! She could sense when there would be lingering issues in the morning.

.   .   .

HOWEVER, despite the mess I may have made today, I'm reminded that God offers me a fresh start every morning to make things right. His mercies are renewed daily – each day brings a brand new opportunity. Why not extend that same chance to your family? Even if there were conflicts today, strive to begin afresh tomorrow.

ONE OF THE most beautiful aspects of marriage is having someone who loves you unconditionally. When Betty and I got married, I weighed a mere 145 pounds. Since then, I've fluctuated from 270 pounds down to my current weight. My son humorously remarks that all the muscles I had fell down around my belt line! Yet, amidst these changes, whether I'm at 145 or 270, or where I am today, I'm still loved unconditionally.

Get rid of the very root of bitterness.

> Looking diligently lest any man fail of the grace of God; **lest any root of bitterness springing up trouble *you*, and thereby many be defiled;** Hebrews 12:15.

If you've ever tended to a garden, you know the critical task of not uprooting weeds completely. Merely trimming a weed won't suffice; until you delve deep and extract the root system, that weed will persistently resurface. Bitterness operates similarly.

ELIMINATING ITS FOUNDATION IS CRUCIAL. You can't afford to let it take root even in its initial stages.

Until You Yank Out the Roots,

The Weed Will Spring Back Up!

DON'T CLING TO RESENTMENT! Attempting to bury an offense under the surface or pretending it never happened won't suffice; you must eliminate the roots! In many marriages and relationships, we may display outward signs of reconciliation and move forward, yet deep down, a seed of bitterness may take hold.

IF LEFT UNCHECKED, bitterness will thrive with each nourishing thought until it dominates the garden of your heart. We've all encountered bitter individuals whose every thought revolves around past wrongs inflicted upon them. While most of us may not reach that extreme, some struggle to think about family without instantly feeling bitterness.

PERHAPS YOU FIND it challenging to forgive at this moment. Maybe you anticipate being more open to forgiveness in the future, but not right now. However, consider Jesus' example when He was on the cross. Despite the agony, He didn't postpone forgiveness. Instead, He immediately pleaded with God to forgive those who wronged Him:

"Father, forgive them" Luke 23:34

THIS EXEMPLIFIES INSTANT FORGIVENESS, asking for forgiveness at that very moment, not delaying it until a more convenient time.

Biblical Forgiveness

If you've been a parent, chances are you've experienced at least one challenging moment. Perhaps not an entire day – if you have perfect kids, that's wonderful! But for most of us, there's been at least one minute of frustration, anxiety, or disappointment. Maybe I'm the only one who's felt this way, and your kids may have never upset, hurt, or angered you. Yet, many parents have had moments when they've wished the ground would swallow up their children!

I HAD one of those "fatherly talks" with my son—you know, the kind —the ones that make you want to pull your hair out! I addressed his habit of breaking speed records on the road, hoping he'd learn to slow down. The Georgia state highway patrolmen issuing him tickets shared my sentiments!

PREDICTABLY, my son fired back with the typical teenage response: "I'm the one dealing with the consequences! Why should you even care?" His reaction left him quite upset, and as he left that night, my wife reassured him, "Your daddy worries because he cares about you."

THERE HAVE BEEN times when I've felt like my own kids couldn't stand me. Moments when I couldn't help but recall every mistake they'd made. "You can't forgive!" they've accused, and at times, I've silently agreed, thinking, "You have no idea how challenging it is!"

PERHAPS I'M the only one facing these struggles. I often wish I had a family like yours – free of problems, arguments, and in-law issues. It must be nice! However, the reality is that most of us need to learn the art of forgiveness. It's the cornerstone of sustaining any meaningful relationship.

.   .   .

Hatred stirreth up strifes: But **love covereth all sins.** Proverbs 10:12

LOVE IS NOT MERELY A FEELING; it's a series of actions. Instead of asking, "What is love?" we should inquire, "What does love do?" Sometimes, a mother wakes up to prepare food for her family, only to have a three-year-old throw it on the floor and in her hair. She may not feel overflowing love for her child in that instant, but she continues demonstrating what love does. She understands that love is a force that operates through her, regardless of how challenging the situation or how wrong the loved one's actions may be. Deep in her heart, she covers her child's unlovable behavior with the genuine forgiveness of love.

SIMILARLY, our holy God displayed immense love by sending His only Son to die for us. This act of love took action and covered our offenses.

Love Is An Action, Not An Emotion

JESUS CHRIST PAID a debt that He didn't owe. His love bore the consequences for others' faults. Sometimes, we are hurt and find ourselves completely innocent – we didn't do anything wrong. However, let's not rush to anger; that's precisely what Christ did for us.

.   .   .

INDEED, biblical forgiveness is about settling the debts of those who have wronged us. If you truly love someone, take proactive steps to address the issues that drive you apart. Once resolved, refrain from revisiting past grievances repeatedly. Fixing relationship problems means moving forward without constantly dredging up each other's pasts.

IN POLITICAL SPHERES, relationships often revolve around adversarial dynamics, where one side opposes the other, and deals are made primarily for self-gain. Politicians relish uncovering dirt from opponents' backgrounds. However, such an approach won't foster a happy marriage. To cultivate a harmonious marriage, both parties must unite and leave their backgrounds behind.

TO TRULY FORGIVE OTHERS, you must first experience genuine forgiveness yourself. Human forgiveness pales compared to divine forgiveness, which is always available upon sincere request. Despite our imperfections, God's forgiveness is unwaveringly present for all who seek it. Just believe.

You Can't Learn To Forgive Until You've Been Truly Forgiven Yourself!

EVEN IF YOU feel unworthy of forgiveness, remember that God welcomes you with open arms, ready to extend His forgiveness. Accepting His forgiveness is the first step in restoring relationships. Confessing our need for God's forgiveness and sincerely seeking it leads to reconciliation and renewed fellowship.

. . .

FORGIVENESS IS the key to restoring joy in every relationship. We must learn to offer true and complete forgiveness to those we love to avoid deep-seated hurt and ongoing conflicts. The Word of God provides the solution, paving the way for a healthy and fulfilling marriage and fulfilling the relationships we desire when we embrace and extend forgiveness.

* * *

Let's Review

1. True forgiveness excuses the offense, though we are offended.
2. True forgiveness separates the offense from the offender.
3. True forgiveness doesn't remember the offense.
4. True forgiveness erases offenses from the record.
5. True forgiveness doesn't mention the offense again.

Quotes for Meditation

True forgiveness breaks a man, and he must forgive.
David Martyn Lloyd-Jones

But graciousness is withholding certain facts you know to be true, so as to leave your enemy's reputation unscathed. Graciousness is shown by what you don't say, even if what you could say would be true. R. T. Kendall

The voice of sin may be loud, but the voice of forgiveness is louder. Dwight L. Moody

Forgiveness is better than revenge, for forgiveness is the sign of a gentle nature, but revenge is the sign of a savage nature. Epictetus

The most marvelous ingredient in the forgiveness of God is that he also forgets, the one thing a human being can never do. Forgetting with God is a divine attribute; God's forgiveness forgets. Oswald Chambers

2

WHAT DOES THE BIBLE WORD
FORGIVE MEAN?

I have added this study just for your personal interest and growth. Originally this was posted as an article on my blog. It got very positive response. I pray it will bless you.

STUDY the word forgive with me to learn what Jesus meant when He told us to forgive as we have been forgiven.

*And **forgive** us our debts, as we **forgive** our debtors. Matthew 6:12.*

THE GREEK WORD behind this word forgive is defined in a Greek lexicon[1] or dictionary in the following ways:

Forgiving is separating something or someone from:

The base root of the word is to cause someone or something to **undergo separation.** That is the meaning of what happens when

God forgives our sins. God separates us from our sins as far as the East is from the West. Psalm 103:12

WHEN WE FORGIVE SOMEONE, we employ the same word, or at least God does. **We are to forgive others as He, God, has forgiven us.** So, we separate what they did from who they are. We decide not to see them in their sin against us but with the eyes of one who has had the love of God shed abroad or poured in our hearts.

JOSEPH FORGAVE his brothers because he could see that God had a purpose in the evil they had done to him. He moved his eyes from their offense to God's purpose.

Forgiving means dismissing or releasing someone or something from a place or one's presence.

That is what God the Father did for us.

- He has **dismissed** our sin from us.
- God has **released us** from the penalty of our sin.
- He has **washed and cleansed us.**
- Our sin is **what we were, but not what we are.** Our sins were horribly dirty, but
- He has **cleansed us.** Isaiah 1:18. He **transformed** us into new creatures, making old things disappear and everything become new.

The word forgive means to

- **undergo separation,**
- **let go,**
- **send away, and**

- **to give up.** It is the same word used for
- **divorce.** It means to release from legal or moral obligation or consequence. It means
- **canceling,**
- **remitting, or**
- **pardoning,** as in a loan. The king forgave 10,000 talents. Matthew 18:24

Forgive is the **remission** of the guilt, the debt of sin. It is being **absolved** of our misdeeds.

THIS IS EXACTLY what God has done for every believer through the cross of Jesus Christ. He has

- **moved our sin away.** He has
- **separated us** from our sin so that
- He doesn't see our sin. Our sin has
- **departed from us.** It left as it did with the demons that left the possessed child. Luke 9:42.

The word is used to speak of

- **giving up or**
- **abandoning.** It means to
- **leave behind** and go on to something else. It is the idea of
- **leaving something in its place without being concerned about it.** It is about
- **letting go,**
- **allowing,**
- **tolerating, and**

- **distancing ourselves** from it.

How is this same word translated in other verses of the New Testament?

The following verses have a word or words in bold that come from the same Greek word. I will provide you with only a few examples of the verses where the word is used. The New Testament uses the word in different forms well over 100 times. The following series of verses let you see how the translators used that Greek word.

AND JESUS ANSWERING said unto him,

- **Suffer** *it*

to be so now: for thus it becometh us to fulfil all righteousness. Then

- **he suffered him. Matthew 3:15**

THEN THE DEVIL

- **leaveth**

him, and, behold, angels came and ministered unto him. Matthew 4:11.

AND THEY STRAIGHTWAY

- **left**

their nets, and followed him. Matthew 4:20.

- **Leave**

THERE THY GIFT before the altar, and go thy way; first be reconciled to thy brother, and then come and offer thy gift. Matthew 5:24

AND IF ANY man will sue thee at the law, and take away thy coat,

- **let him have**

thy cloke also. Matthew 5:40

BUT JESUS SAID UNTO HIM, Follow me; and

- **let**

the dead bury their dead. Matthew 8:22.

THEN JESUS

- **sent the multitude away,**

and went into the house: and his disciples came unto him, saying, Declare unto us the parable of the tares of the field. Matthew 13:36

THEN ANSWERED Peter and said unto him, Behold, we

- **have forsaken**

all, and followed thee; what shall we have therefore? Matthew 19:27

WOE UNTO YOU, scribes and Pharisees, hypocrites! for ye pay tithe of mint and anise and cummin, and have

- **omitted the**

weightier *matters* of the law, judgment, mercy, and faith: these ought ye to have done, and not to

- **leave the other undone.**

Matthew 23:23

AND LIKEWISE ALSO THE MEN,

- **leaving**

the natural use of the woman, burned in their lust one toward another; men with men working that which is unseemly, and receiving in themselves that recompence of their error which was meet. Romans 1:27

BUT AND IF SHE DEPART,

- **let**

her remain unmarried, or be reconciled to *her* husband: and let not the husband

- **put away**

his wife. 1 Corinthians 7:11.

NEVERTHELESS I HAVE *SOMEWHAT* against thee, because thou

- **hast left**

thy first love. Revelation 2:4

~

WHAT GOD DID when He forgave us

ALL YOU READ in the definition above explains what happened when God forgave us. You know the verses and what the Bible says about your sin. You know without this article that the believer's sins have been.

- blotted out,
- are no longer remembered,
- cleansed,
- cast into the depths of the sea,
- moved from us as far away as the East is from the West,
- forgiven, and
- nailed to the cross. There is more; our sins have been
- made as white as snow,
- covered,
- canceled, and
- paid in full. He
- passes over our sins. He never thinks of us and our sin in the same thought. Our sins and past are
- passed away.

- Our sins have been placed on Jesus.
- I am sure you are thinking of something I have forgotten.

What God expects us to do with our forgiveness?

We are to forgive others just like we have been forgiven.

And be ye kind one to another, tenderhearted, forgiving one another, **even as God for Christ's sake hath forgiven you. Ephesians 4:32**

Then came Peter to him, and said, Lord, how oft shall my brother sin against me, and I forgive him? till seven times? 22 Jesus saith unto him, I say not unto thee, **Until seven times: but, Until seventy times seven.** Matthew 18:21-22

Forbearing one another, and forgiving one another, if any man have a quarrel against any: **even as Christ forgave you, so also** *do* ye. Colossians 3:13

- Having explored various definitions of the word, we then reflected on how God extends forgiveness to us. This understanding illuminates His expectation for us to forgive others. Indeed, the forgiven are called to forgive—a fundamental principle in the Bible. Failure or reluctance to forgive may suggest a misalignment with God's family. Love, as taught in Scripture, originates from God.

Quotes for Meditation

You forgive me, and I forgive you, and we forgive them, and they forgive us, and so a circle of unlimited forbearance and love goes round the world. Charles Spurgeon

The man who does not forgive has never been forgiven, but the man who has been freely forgiven at once forgives others. Charles Spurgeon

Unforgiving people have not been forgiven themselves; those who are forgiven are so broken by it that they cannot but forgive others. David Martyn Lloyd-Jones

We need not climb up into heaven to see whether our sins are forgiven; let us look into our hearts, and see if we can forgive others. If we can, we need not doubt but God has forgiven us. Thomas Watson

"I can forgive, but I cannot forget," is only another way of saying, "I will not forgive." Anonymous

One of the old German devotional philosophers took the position that God loves to forgive big sins more than He does little sins because the bigger the sin, the more glory accrues to Him for his forgiveness. I remember the writer went on to say that not only does God forgive sins and enjoy doing it, but as soon as He has forgiven them, He forgets them and trusts the person just as if he or she had never sinned. I share his view that God not only forgives great sins as readily as little ones, but once He has forgiven them He starts anew right there and never brings up the old sins again....

When a person makes a mistake and has to be forgiven, the shadow may hang over him or her because it is hard for other people to forget. But when God forgives, He begins the new page right there, and then the devil runs up and says, "What about this person's past?" God replies: "What past? There is no past. We started out fresh when he came to Me and I forgave him!" A. W. Tozer[2]

---

1. *A Greek-English Lexicon of the New Testament and Other Early Christian Literature*
2. *A. W. Tozer, Faith Beyond Reason,* 113.

3

LEARNING TO LOVE FIRST

We love him, because **he first loved us.** I John 4:19

Every love relationship starts with someone taking the initiative. It requires stepping out of one's comfort zone and making the first move to initiate the connection.

OVER FIFTY YEARS AGO, I unexpectedly encountered a girl sporting long, hippy-style hair sitting on a curb. I had been working on a friend's car and just ran by her. I noticed her but tried to act like I didn't, you know.

IN MY SUBSEQUENT encounter with her, a group from college was going out to get a bite. We had Rick as the "designated driver" for a group that night, and he owned the most impressive car in our school – a 1947 Plymouth famous throughout our college town of Rome, Georgia. Our outing was for pizza, and we all piled into Rick's car. He sat in the driver's seat with Betty next to him in the middle, leaving me, the Tennessee redneck, in the middle back seat. Being the designated driver only means the Rick was driving because we all liked his car.

AS THE NIGHT CONCLUDED, and Rick parked the car back on campus, everyone began to exit the vehicle. Betty and I were the last ones in line to get out in the middle of the front and back seats. However, I had other plans in mind. Instead of stepping out of the car like everyone else, I seized the opportunity, jumped into the front seat, and drove off with both the vehicle and the girl!

I FOUND HER CUTE AND, mustering up courage, asked her for a double date with my friends Jürgen and Sally. Surprisingly, she accepted my invitation! That night, as I sat in the car with Betty, I was excited to be on a date with such a beautiful girl!

I ATTEMPTED ALL the classic moves to get closer to her during the date, like the stretch-yawn trick to put my arm around her casually. However, it felt more like hugging a block of ice!

AS IT TURNED OUT, Betty wasn't actually interested in me. She had her eye on my friend Jürgen and saw our date as a means of getting closer to him.

DESPITE THE INITIAL SETBACK, our subsequent dates took a different turn! I was determined not to repeat that awkward experience. If I were going to try to have a date with someone like Betty, I wouldn't let another guy spoil it for me!

· · ·

DESPITE MY EFFORTS, it didn't initially seem like Betty was particularly interested in me. In fact, after our first date, she wrote to her mother, saying, "I just went out with a pretty nice guy, but he's a bit of a redneck." However, despite her reservations, she's been my wife for well over 50 years now! It's all because I took the initiative to start the love between us.

Initiating love first is effective!

Living together inevitably brings challenges. No matter how strong the love between two people, close proximity often leads to occasional conflicts.

HAVE you ever experienced a prolonged argument that took days to resolve? Perhaps your household is always harmonious, but let's be realistic—disagreements happen. Even if the newlyweds haven't disagreed yet, they will soon! It remains to be seen how they navigate challenges as soon as the honeymoon phase is over.

Loving First Really Works!

EVERY RELATIONSHIP eventually reaches a point where the second principle of creating a healthy and fulfilling marriage becomes crucial – a dedication to loving each other first, even amidst disagreements or conflicts.

How God Loved First

When counseling husbands and wives, it's common for the husband to express his desire to solve problems by saying, "I love her, and I'm committed to making things right, but she needs to fix some things FIRST." Similarly, when turning to the wife, she often responds, "I'm ready to work on our relationship, but FIRST, he needs to change this!"

THEY'RE both waiting for the other to take the first step, which has made their home a battleground, their family unhappy, and their marriage cold and lifeless. Neither is willing to take the necessary initiative to resolve their issues.

BUT LET'S reflect on Christ's love. What does a healthy and fulfilling marriage look like? Who takes the initiative in our relationship with God? We discover He consistently loves FIRST at every stage of our relationship with Him.

THIS CONCEPT IS EXPLAINED to us in I John 4:19:

We love Him because He first loved us.

WE'RE in love with God today because He took the initiative to love us first! He loved when we didn't deserve it and we still do not.

SOME INDIVIDUALS SEEK to reconcile with God by believing they need to find Him and make amends. However, the Bible teaches that we cannot initiate love or seek God first because He has already demonstrated His love by giving Himself for us. There was a great gulf stretched between God and man.

·   ·   ·

THERE WAS an insurmountable gap between humanity and God. Recognizing this, God made the pivotal decision: "I love people and desire a personal relationship with them so that I will extend my love to them first." Jesus exemplified this by choosing to love first, paving the way for restored, personal fellowship with God.

SOME BELIEVE they can earn God's love by obeying religious practices and doing good deeds. They meticulously observe dietary restrictions, observe certain days, and lead morally upright lives, all in pursuit of God's love. However, true love is not found in our actions but in what God has already done for us.

> Herein is love, not that we loved God, but that He loved us... I John 4:10

GOD'S LOVE for us is unparalleled – He sent His only Son into the world to address our problems, demonstrating the depth of His love. Salvation isn't contingent on our actions, a church's actions, or religious rituals, but on what Christ has already accomplished for us! Religion often revolves around attempting to earn God's favor, leading people across various cultures to devise extreme measures to reconcile with God. From offering human sacrifices to engaging in extreme fasting and self-harm, these efforts aim to earn God's love somehow. However, the truth is that salvation doesn't originate from our efforts to love God; rather, it stems from God's decision to love us unconditionally.

THE BIBLE unequivocally declares that God loved us long before we even considered loving Him! His message is clear: "I will send My only Son to pay the ultimate price for your eternal life. Despite your countless mistakes, I will welcome you into My family and call you My sons and daughters."

RELIGION NOT GOD often presents a narrative of uncertainty, saying, "I cannot determine your fate after death. I'll assess your good deeds against your bad ones to predict your outcome. Therefore, I advise you to perform good deeds and follow strict rules just to be safe. Earn as many 'brownie points' as possible to please God." Sadly, many adopt this mindset when approaching our relationship with God.

HOWEVER, God's message is vastly different. He declares, "You may have faltered, messed up, slipped, but I love you unconditionally. You don't need to achieve perfection; I will make things right for you."

THE FUNDAMENTAL QUESTION arises in our relationships: "Who will take the initiative? Who will make the first move to restore the relationship? How can we mend our broken relationships with our parents, friends, spouse, or children?" It requires someone to step up and be the first to love.

If You Won Their Heart Once, You Can Do It Again!

MOST OF US genuinely have loving marriages and relationships. Despite occasional feelings of failure or discord, the desire to improve and nurture our connections is inherent within us. We often get along harmoniously with our loved ones. However, even in the most loving marriages, tension and disagreement exist. Experiencing division with the most important people in our lives is distressing. Yet, if you won your spouse's heart once, you can do it again! If you witnessed your partner falling in love with you previously, it can happen again! Similarly, you can regain your children's affection and acceptance. But achieving this requires a steadfast commitment to love them first.

Undeserved Love

Do you remember the early days of dating your spouse? It felt like everything about them was perfect! Guys meticulously polished their shoes, brushed their teeth, and ensured their breath was fresh. They went out of their way to be ideal gentlemen, opening doors and charming you in every way. It might have felt like they swept you off your feet!

HOWEVER, how swiftly can things change after the wedding ceremony? Once you've been married for some time, you are often (quite abruptly) introduced to the real person. It turns out that even the "knights in shining armor" wake up with bad moods and bad breath! The truth is, it took hours of effort to maintain that polished persona they used to be! And then you begin to understand why their momma may have wanted to get rid of them so badly! Sooner or later, you realize that the person you love is human, with their own set of flaws and imperfections.

IF SOMEONE DESERVES your love today, it doesn't necessarily mean they will deserve it tomorrow. That's why real love must persevere even when it's not deserved.

THIS IS the essence of how God chooses to love us.

. . .

PERHAPS YOU SOMETIMES ENTERTAIN THE thought that God would love you more if you were a better person. "If only I could quit drinking. Suppose I could cease engaging in premarital sex if I could be more truthful. If I could improve my behavior, maybe God could extend His love to me!"

BUT ROMANS 5:6 and 8 tells us that God loved us and Jesus died for us when we couldn't do anything to help ourselves, when we were wicked, and still sinning sinners.

> For when we were yet **without strength** (didn't have the strength to get right with God), in due time (right on time) Christ died for the **ungodly** (those that were nothing like Him). Romans 5:6.

> But God commendeth (showed, demonstrated) his love toward us, in that, while we were **yet sinners,** (still sinning sinners) Christ died for us. Romans 5:8.

GOD DIDN'T WAIT for us to clean ourselves up! Even on our worst days, when we struggled, God's love for us was unwavering. He loved us enough to sacrifice His life for us without expecting us to have everything figured out or to be perfect. Despite our shortcomings and mistakes, He chose to give Himself for us! None of us can honestly claim to deserve such love, yet God offers it freely to all. Isn't that astonishing?

> And you *hath he quickened (made alive)*, who were **dead** (cut off or separated) **in trespasses and sins;** Ephesians 2:1.

THE BIBLE USES another relationship term to describe the state of affairs between us and God: "dead." This term signifies a severed communication, much like picking up a dead phone that's unable to make calls or establish any form of communication. Sin acts as the disruptor, cutting off our connection to God and leaving us spiritually dead, with no way to bridge the gap to Heaven. However, God takes the initiative to repair this broken connection and restore communication with Heaven.

WE ALL UNDERSTAND the concept of a severed line of communication, especially in marriage. Many of us have experienced the challenging dynamics of the "silent treatment." It's a phase where communication completely stops, and couples find themselves emotionally disconnected. When communication breaks down to this extent, it can pave the way for separation and divorce. The key to resolving communication issues in marriage lies in one spouse taking the initiative to break the silence and restore the bond of fellowship.

YOU MIGHT HAVE GONE through significant hurt in your relationship. It's a reality that divorce and separation are prevalent issues in America. I recall when Betty was studying psychology in college, and shortly after we got married, her instructor mentioned that the two-year mark often sees a peak in divorce rates. This information left her feeling anxious, fearing that challenges were imminent. Perhaps you've faced callous times in your own home. Despite these challenges, remember that you still have the power to love. Even when options are running thin in your relationship, choosing to love first can make a significant difference.

IT'S NOT about proving who's right or wrong; it's about who's willing to invest in love. Repairing a marriage requires someone to sacrifice and pay the price for love. Love isn't just a feeling; it's an active choice and commitment. If you base your understanding of love on a "Holly-wood" portrayal, you'll likely be misled because their romantic narratives rarely reflect real and enduring love.

I REMEMBER WATCHING an episode of "My Three Sons" where the oldest son believed he had found true love because he imagined wedding scenes whenever he saw the girl. However, real love doesn't operate solely on romantic feelings. Love is more than just an emotional response; it's about consistent actions and choices, especially during challenging times.

IN REALITY, love isn't solely based on fleeting emotions. It's about making deliberate decisions to show love, even when circumstances are challenging. True love endures beyond momentary feelings; it remains steadfast even when faced with difficulties. To love my wife as Christ does means choosing to love unconditionally, regardless of whether it's deserved or reciprocated at every moment.

Proactive love

> Charity (undeserved love) suffereth long, (is patient) *and* is kind; charity (undeserved love) envieth not; charity (undeserved love) vaunteth not itself, (doesn't brag) is not puffed up, (not haughty) 5 Doth not behave itself unseemly, (good manners) seeketh not her own, (not selfish) is not easily provoked, (not mad easily) thinketh no evil; 6 Rejoiceth not in iniquity, but rejoiceth in the truth; 7 Beareth all things, believeth all things, hopeth all things, endureth all things. 1 Corinthians 13:4–7.

In 1 Corinthians 13:5, we learn that love does not entertain negative thoughts. Love is inherently positive and refrains from thinking ill of others. However, when relationship issues arise, it's easy to fall into a negative thinking pattern.

HAVE you ever found yourself replaying a conversation in your mind, dissecting every word and action, and painting scenarios of betrayal or malice? It's like conversing with yourself, questioning why the other person said or did something, and dwelling on past grievances. This internal dialogue can quickly spiral into feelings of self-pity or even thoughts of retaliation. What's happening in these moments? You're allowing negative thoughts to take root and grow, poisoning your perspective on your loved one.

Love Doesn't Feel; It Does

LOVE, on the other hand, operates differently. It chooses to focus on the positive aspects of the relationship and gives the benefit of the doubt. Love doesn't jump to conclusions or assume the worst about someone's intentions. It seeks understanding and reconciliation rather than dwelling on perceived wrongs.

So, when faced with relationship challenges, guarding against negative thinking is crucial. Instead of letting your mind wander into suspicion or resentment, choose to approach the situation with love and a positive outlook. This mindset shift can make a significant difference in resolving conflicts and maintaining healthy relationships.

· · ·

WE OFTEN CATCH ourselves in moments of frustration, thinking, "How can they treat me like this, especially after all I've done?" It's easy to let bitterness seep in and convince ourselves that retaliation or resentment is justified. Our thoughts become poisoned, tarnishing our view of the person we love.

HOWEVER, the essence of true love lies in refusing to harbor negative thoughts, regardless of the circumstances. This mirrors the example set by Christ Himself. In Jeremiah 29:11, God assures us of His thoughts of peace and goodwill toward us, despite our shortcomings. God's love transcends our faults and failures, always seeking our well-being.

> For I know the thoughts that I think toward you, saith the Lord, **thoughts of peace, and not of evil, to give you an expected end.**
> Jeremiah 29:11

LIKEWISE, we should strive to emulate this mindset in our relationships. Instead of dwelling on flaws and past disagreements, we should focus on the good we can bring to each other's lives. The world's concept of love often hinges on self-interest, expecting something in return. However, God's love is selfless and unconditional, even to those with nothing to offer in return.

So, let us choose to rise above negative thoughts and embrace a mindset of love and positivity. By doing so, we honor God's example and nurture healthier and more fulfilling relationships with those we cherish.

. . .

I CORINTHIANS 13 continues to teach us that love is selfless; it

"does not seek its own."

PERSONAL GAIN, desires, or past wounds don't drive it. On the contrary, selfish love is shackled by these very things, always looking out for its own interests and needs. This self-centered love is often the root cause of strife in homes and pain in marriages.

Here are some examples of selfish love in action:

• A husband who only loves his wife for the chores she does without appreciation.

• A wife who loves her husband solely for his financial provision and care.

• Parents who withhold blessings from their children for their own pleasure.

• Children who love their parents only because they fulfill their desires.

• A person who loves their partner only for physical intimacy.

Now, let's delve into the transformative power of loving first. Embracing this principle can lead us to extraordinary actions and resolutions. When was the last time you took ownership of a mistake and sincerely apologized to your spouse or child? Demanding that others fix things is easy, but true love takes responsibility for healing rifts.

INSTEAD OF ADOPTING A "ME-FIRST" attitude, imagine saying, "I'm sorry. I realize I was wrong, and I'm committed to making things right." This requires humility and genuine care for the well-being of your loved ones.

CONTRAST this with the common scenario where egos clash, and each person waits for the other to make amends. However, this standoffish approach never aligns with God's love. He loved us unconditionally, even when we didn't deserve it or reciprocate it.

You Can Solve Any Marriage Problem You's Got!

WHAT IF YOU responded to negativity and hurt with an outpouring of love instead? What if every hurtful word or deed was met with kindness and understanding? The Bible tells us that love is unconquerable; no amount of negativity can extinguish it.

So, challenge yourself to love without conditions or expectations. Your family may resist at first, but they'll eventually yield to the overwhelming force of unconditional love. Love that doesn't seek its own but seeks to mend, nurture, and uplift.

AFTER OVER FIVE decades of personal experience and deep dives into the Bible, I can confidently assert that any marital issue can be resolved. The key lies in making the decision to lead with love, regardless of how it's reciprocated. Love has an incredible power that makes it challenging to resist.

.   .   .

HAVE you ever experienced a moment when your child or grandchild hesitated to embrace your outstretched arms? It can be quite painful. Yet, if you persist in showering them with love, they eventually find solace in your embrace.

HOWEVER, in marriage, instead of covering a fault with love, we often respond with a single hurtful word. This triggers a chain reaction where each response escalates the conflict. Sadly, we witness family tragedies in the news regularly, stemming from the absence of proactive love within households. This underscores the crucial need for someone to take the initiative and love first.

THE MOST CRUCIAL realization we can have is that God holds the answers to our marriage, business, and family challenges. By knowing Him personally, you gain access to these solutions and more. You don't need to search for Him or struggle to love Him – He has already taken care of everything for you! His provision covers every problem and fulfills every need.

PERHAPS YOU'RE unfamiliar with the personal love of God, unsure of His forgiveness and what consequences await your sins. But rest assured, God is always ready to extend forgiveness, even when we don't deserve it.

JUST LIKE HOW Betty initially had doubts about me but ended up marrying me, demonstrating that even the unexpected can happen, love has the power to overcome relationship issues that linger in your household. By taking the first step and loving unconditionally, you can triumph over these challenges.

Review

1. God loved us when we were totally unworthy.
2. We did nothing to earn his love.
3. He took the first step
4. He loves us even when we are unlovely
5. This is an example of how we must love in our marriage if we desire to have a health and fulfilling marriage.

4

SACRIFICING YOURSELF

I n the previous chapters, we delved into the issues that selfishness introduces into relationships. Moving forward, we'll explore a principle that acts as selfishness's antithesis, a cornerstone in building a "healthy and fulfilling marriage" of relationships. This principle is encapsulated in the verse that serves as our blueprint,

Husbands, love your wives, even as Christ also loved the church, and gave himself for it; Ephesians 5:25.

Selfishness Is An Inability To Deny Our Own Selves

PAUL PRESENTS us with a profound paradigm shift in how we approach love in our relationships, urging us to imitate Christ's love in how we treat others. This perspective introduces us to a key concept: love is inherently tied to the act of giving. Love, in its purest form, cannot be separated from this commitment to give. This is vividly illustrated in Christ's ultimate sacrifice for the church and further echoed in John 3:16, which reinforces the link between love and the act of giving:

> "For God so loved the world that He gave His one and only Son..."

SELFISHNESS STEMS from an inability to look beyond our own desires, even at the expense of hurting others. Conversely, self-sacrifice is the capacity to extend ourselves for the benefit of another, regardless of the personal cost. This selfless giving is the very essence of love, transforming our relationships into reflections of divine love.

Evidence of the Problem of Selfishness

Self-centeredness is a glaring manifestation of the fundamental sin issue permeating our world. The pervasive message across media platforms, from television and radio to seminars and literature, champions the ethos of prioritizing oneself above all else. This cultural narrative constantly reinforces the importance of meeting one's own needs first. However, the teachings of the Bible present a starkly contrasting perspective on how we should navigate relationships, advocating for a shift from selfishness to selflessness.

THE DEMISE of many marriages can be traced back to issues rooted in selfishness, a problem that also spells the end for numerous friendships. At the core of most interpersonal conflicts is the presence of self-centeredness: a staunch adherence to personal opinions and methodologies coupled with a readiness to contend for their supremacy. Yet, for those who aspire to build a "healthy and fulfilling marriage" of harmonious and fulfilling relationships, a critical juncture arrives—a point where adopting a different, more selfless approach becomes imperative.

THE INSIDIOUS NATURE of selfishness often manifests itself within our marriages in various ways, with financial disputes being a prime example. Reflecting on the early days of my marriage, I recall the humorous yet telling quarrels about money between us and another couple, close friends of ours. Whenever my friend and I decided to grab a quick meal, he would go to great lengths to conceal the expenditure from his wife, fearing the inevitable claim of an equivalent amount for her personal use. Similarly, if our wives indulged in a modest shopping spree, spending, let's say, ten dollars on shoes, there was an unspoken rule that this expenditure must remain a secret among them. The fear was that disclosure would automatically entitle their husbands to an equivalent discretionary spending.

Fighting over money

This might sound amusing, yet it underscores a deeper issue that isn't exclusive to them or to us. Betty and I, too, have faced our fair share of disagreements where money was the focal point—debates over ownership of the funds, entitlements to spending, judgments on who spends more wisely, or who is to blame for the depletion of our financial resources. These are not merely petty squabbles but are indicative of underlying selfish impulses that challenge the harmony of a relationship.

Whose Fault Was Your Last Speeding Ticket?

Making decisions based on personal comfort

THE PURSUIT of personal comfort often becomes a dominating principle in our decision-making, leading us to make choices that prioritize our own ease and convenience, sometimes at the expense of those closest to us. This self-centered approach can manifest in various scenarios, from trivial daily choices to significant life decisions. The tendency to evaluate options through the lens of personal benefit without considering the impact on our partner or family can sow discord and resentment. In relationships where both parties adopt a "survival of the fittest" stance, the dynamics can devolve into a territorial dispute over resources and decisions, with each person defensively guarding their own interests to avoid being overshadowed by the other's selfishness. This mindset contributes significantly to conflicts within the home, as it shifts the focus from mutual support and shared goals to competition for personal gain and comfort.

Blaming others for failures

It seems we have a knack for dodging responsibility, especially when things go awry in our family dynamics. It's almost a running joke in my household that if something's amiss, it must be Betty's doing. Convincing me otherwise? Good luck! We're rather tightfisted in doling out credit but lavish in distributing blame. This penchant for shifting blame isn't new; it's as old as humanity itself. Recall the first wrongdoing in Eden—Adam and Eve were quick to point fingers, initiating a legacy of deflection.

CONSIDER THIS: who did you fault for your last speeding ticket? Caught by the surprise of flashing lights, did you curse the sudden drop in speed limit or label it a speed trap, conveniently ignoring that glaring sign you zoomed past? It's almost comedic how every traffic stop feels like a setup—at least from my seat behind the wheel. This tendency to assign blame elsewhere, even to those closest to us, is ingrained in our nature.

WE'RE experts at concocting excuses for our behaviors, attitudes, or thoughts. Modern psychology has profited handsomely by providing justifications for our actions. It's never our fault, right? Perhaps it's all because of some bizarre prenatal influence—like your mother's peculiar encounter with a pig during pregnancy. The narrative is always the same: "It's not my fault; it's due to circumstances beyond my control." The thought of bearing the blame ourselves? Unthinkable. It's much easier to find a scapegoat, sparing us the discomfort of self-reflection and admission of fault.

Desiring everything to revolve around self

We've all encountered that individual who craves the spotlight, needing everything to orbit around them. Whether it's the demanding relative at family gatherings insisting everyone try Aunt Susie's casserole or else face familial discord or moments in our own marriages where differing preferences collide, it often boils down to a clash of egos: "My way because I matter most." While we may not articulate it so bluntly, what else but an inflated sense of self-importance could fuel such conflicts over seemingly trivial matters?

THE NOTION of giving with an ulterior motive is often misunderstood as a means to achieve personal gains. However, this kind of giving is just as self-serving as not giving at all. Behind these acts of generosity often lurk hidden agendas. For instance, some individuals may believe that by giving to their spouse, they earn the right to demand what they want in return. Similarly, others may assume that they can secure future favor from their partners by making concessions in the present. These forms of giving are tainted with selfishness, driven by personal interests rather than genuine, unconditional love for one's spouse.

Giving to Get

In Peru, a saying perfectly captures this mindset of transactional giving: "Hoy por ti; mañana por mi," which translates to "Today for you, tomorrow for me." It reflects the idea of expecting reciprocation after giving, but in reality, that "tomorrow" of reciprocation often never arrives. Such attitudes reveal that the initial act of giving was primarily focused on self-care, and the promise of future consideration is usually forgotten. Many of us fall into this trap of believing that giving today grants us the right to be selfish in the future.

RECALL the effort and dedication you poured into making your partner feel cherished and valued before marriage. You strived to ensure they felt loved and appreciated with every gesture. Why not revive that genuine, selfless giving in your relationship today?

Expectations

Expectations can be one of the most detrimental aspects in relationships with friends and family. Have you ever caught yourself thinking along these lines: "My birthday is approaching, and it's my first year as a pastor after years of missionary work! Surely, they'll remember and shower me with great gifts! The church has some funds, my family is well-off, and some of our members are wealthy too. I'm sure to get a fantastic gift this year!"

Instead of Being Thankful for the $50 I Got,
I Feel Gypped!

. . .

BUT AS SOON AS expectations like these take hold, problems start brewing. Let's say I anticipate receiving $100 (just a hypothetical figure – feel free to send me $1,000 for my birthday!). I base this expectation on knowing that Brother Smith alone could easily manage that amount. So, when my birthday arrives, and Brother Smith hands me a $50 check, what's my reaction? Instead of appreciating the $50, I feel shortchanged and like he's taken $50 from me!

OR CONSIDER performance evaluations at work. You're anticipating a 5% raise; at least, that's what you expect. However, when your boss praises you for a 3% pay increase, are you ecstatic? Probably not. You may express gratitude, but deep down, it feels like a portion of your salary has been snatched away.

SIMILARLY, I might expect my spouse to have dinner ready precisely at 5 p.m. When I return home after a long day, I envision a warm, delicious meal waiting to be enjoyed. But if that expectation isn't met, I'm ready to voice my disappointment!

PERHAPS YOU'VE EXPERIENCED BEING on the other end of these scenarios. You've toiled all day preparing a meal for your family to enjoy together at 5 p.m., only for your partner to stroll in at 7:30 p.m. You greet them with a suggestion to reheat leftovers, leading to disagreements fueled by unmet expectations.

EXPECTING certain actions or behaviors from others because it's what we believe they should do for us can create a significant barrier in friendships. It's akin to mentally placing someone in a debtor's position – they owe us. This tendency is prevalent even among individuals exploring new churches, where the mindset often shifts to "What's in it for me? What can I expect to receive?"

IN THE BIBLE, we learn a profound lesson: despite having nothing to offer God, with Him having no expectations from us, He chose to give Himself for us. What if we applied this selfless giving in our marriages, giving everything we have and are to our spouses without expecting anything in return or getting into arguments about who owes what to whom?

MY OWN SELFISHNESS caused a rift between my wife and me. I came home late after a particularly exhausting day spent surrounded by people, as I do every day. I longed for a few moments of solitude, a rare luxury for me. So, I settled back in bed to watch a crime TV show when my son Chris called. I didn't answer immediately, although I knew it was him from the loud announcement on my phone. I planned to call him back during the next commercial break. Sounds terrible, right? I just wanted my hour - just one hour!

HOWEVER, my wife cannot bear to leave a ringing phone unanswered. For her, every call must be answered because, in her mind, it could be an emergency!

NOW, if it's an emergency, they'll call back, and rushing won't make a difference. Besides, I couldn't possibly get there in time if something serious were happening. So, I politely asked her to let me watch my show in peace.

HOWEVER, Betty (my wife) immediately picked up the phone and started dialing Chris. In frustration, I ordered her to put the phone back (in a loving manner, of course!). Her response was straightforward: "I can't believe you!" and she stormed off.

I KNEW I was in the wrong. The next day, I even wrote her a letter acknowledging my selfish behavior and apologizing. But apologies like mine often come with excuses: "I'm sorry, but can't you understand I just wanted my hour? I was going to call him back right away!"

PERHAPS YOU'VE NEVER HAD a fight like this. Maybe you're already thinking, "This guy has some serious family issues!" But the truth is, selfish expectations can lead to trouble in any relationship, no matter who you are or what your circumstances may be.

Expressions of Self-Sacrifice

Fights in the evening always seem to carry a unique intensity, don't they? That night, I felt like I had a bit of a grace period since the sun had already set. It was as if I had a personal exception clause from God, allowing me to stay mad at Betty for a while longer!

HOWEVER, nothing compares to the joy of being in a relationship where giving to each other is the guiding principle. Sadly, the love we feel in our hearts often fails to translate into our actions. Even if we aspire to be selfless givers, we may struggle to put that intention into practice. So, how can we truly demonstrate self-sacrificing love for each other? How can we bridge the gap between our good intentions and our daily reality?

Seeking to fulfill the desires of others

We find a powerful example of selfless love in the Bible when the Philippian church needed assistance, and the Apostle Paul decided to send his trusted companion Timothy to them. Paul praised Timothy, saying, "Timothy's not like anyone else you know! He'll care for you like you were his own! Timothy's not in this work for what he gets out of it, for his feelings, or for what good things happen to him! He'll care for you and meet your needs!"

Timothy Is Not Like Anyone Else You Know!

IN PHILIPPIANS 2:20-21, Paul elaborated on why Timothy was so exceptional:

> For I **have** no man likeminded, who will naturally **care** for
> your state. **21** For all **seek** their own, not the things
> which are Jesus Christ's.

TIMOTHY's genuine care for others stood out because most people were focused on their own agendas, desires, and pleasures, while Timothy devoted himself to serving others. Anyone who can exhibit such selfless love is indeed extraordinary!

THIS LEVEL of sacrificial love is what we also promised before God at our wedding. I remember witnessing my assistant pastor in Peru, Alonso, getting married a few months before I returned to the States. It was a moving sight as Alonso stood opposite his bride, tears streaming down his cheeks as he made his vows. His new wife tenderly wiped away his tears, and the entire congregation was deeply moved. It was a poignant reminder of the depth of commitment and love we pledge to each other in marriage.

AT TIMES, the emotional fervor of our vows can overshadow their core essence. However, the fundamental message conveyed in most wedding vows encapsulates this profound concept – that prioritizing my spouse's well-being will always take precedence over my personal fulfillment. Our marriage is founded on my commitment to fulfill your needs, not solely my own.

Biting your tongue

> Not rendering evil for evil, or railing for railing: but contrariwise blessing; knowing that ye are thereunto called, that ye should inherit a blessing. I Peter 3:9

Here are some instructions that I found truly valuable the other night! What unfolded that evening with Betty and me, a scenario often repeated in our marriages and relationships, illustrates a common human tendency: when someone wrongs us, our instinct is to retaliate fiercely. If provoked, I'm prone to respond with harshness or even escalate the conflict. However, these instructions remind us not to respond to evil with more evil.

PERHAPS YOU'VE HEARD of the pastor who once conducted marriage counseling for a couple on the brink of constant fighting. He positioned the husband and wife on opposite ends of the room, each armed with a pen and paper. Their task was simple: write down the issues that needed addressing and resolving. The wife, filled with anger, started writing furiously, casting occasional glances of resentment toward her husband. In contrast, the husband sat calmly, a gentle smile playing on his lips. His serene demeanor only seemed to fuel the wife's agitation, intensifying her writing spree.

"Biting Your Tongue" Doesn't Mean NOT Saying What You Want to Say.

AFTER A BRIEF WRITING SESSION, both spouses returned to the pastor's desk. Without hesitation, the pastor picked up the husband's paper and began reading aloud:

"I WANT to express my sincerest apologies. I recognize my faults and shortcomings, and I deeply appreciate the wonderful person she is..."

AT THAT MOMENT, the wife erupted from her seat, demanding, "Please, tear up mine immediately!" It became evident that replacing hateful words with words of kindness and understanding can yield profound transformations in a relationship.

THE CONCEPT OF "RAILING FOR RAILING" refers to exchanging harsh and hurtful words in response to similar treatment. However, transformative moments occur when we choose to respond with blessings instead. Simply holding back hurtful words isn't enough; we must actively replace negative thoughts with words of sweetness and reconciliation before they escape our lips.

Giving with no thought of return

Jesus imparted a profound teaching about hospitality when He encouraged us to invite those who cannot repay us. His message was clear: we should extend kindness and generosity without expecting anything in return. However, it's all too human to fall into the mindset of reciprocity. We might think, "I'll treat you to a hot dog today because that's within my means, and hopefully, you'll reciprocate with a steak dinner later since that's what you can afford." Yet, Christ's teaching challenges us to give freely, devoid of expectations of repayment.

CONSIDER the scenario of a wife dedicating her entire day to preparing a special meal, anticipating a heartfelt expression of gratitude from her husband. She gladly puts in the effort and doesn't mind the stress, all in the hope of receiving appreciation and joy from her husband. She envisions a delightful evening together, filled with warmth and love. However, as dinner approaches, her anticipation is dampened by an unwelcome call from her husband, announcing that he must work late.

SUDDENLY, the love and effort she invested in preparing the meal turned into frustration and disappointment. It becomes evident that her efforts were not solely for the joy of giving but rather an investment in her own happiness, contingent upon a specific response from her husband. However, self-sacrificing love embodies a different ethos—it says, "I am willing to give my all to you, regardless of whether there's a reason to expect anything in return." •

Offering security versus doubt

I've been in ministry for well over 50 years now, and throughout my experience, I've learned that sometimes, the individuals who express the most affection are the quickest to withdraw their support. Del, one of the first young men I mentored for ministry in Peru, was particularly devoted, always claiming the seat beside me and proudly declaring his loyalty. He would often assert, "I'm your right-hand man! Whatever you need, I'm here!" His dedication was admirable, but unfortunately, it didn't last, and one day he abruptly quit.

ENCOUNTERS like this teach us to question the authenticity of relationships around us, including our marriages. Over time, we become skeptical, assuming that our spouse or children have hidden agendas behind their kindness and affection. This skepticism can erode the foundation of trust and love in our marriages.

We Learn To Doubt That People Are Who They Project Themselves To Be!

RECENTLY, a visitor at my church approached me after the service with a curious question: "Are you real?" He clarified, "I mean, are you genuinely who you seem to be?" His inquiry, though light-hearted, reflects the inherent doubt we carry about people's authenticity. However, self-sacrificing love provides the assurance that our love is unconditional and sincere.

I ONCE HEARD about a man who told his wife before leaving on a trip, "If you haven't lost 30 pounds by the time I return, I'll divorce you!" Despite her efforts to meet his demands, their marriage didn't survive. While you might not express demands so explicitly, many of us attach conditions to our love, expecting certain criteria to be met before we give our affection.

. . .

SELF-SACRIFICING LOVE, on the other hand, rejects selfishness. It's the antithesis of demanding or taking; instead, it involves giving and sacrificing our own needs for the sake of our loved ones. For the ultimate example of self-sacrificing love, we look to Christ, who showed us a love that is not based on what we can gain or take but on genuine, sacrificial giving.

The Great Sacrificer

Let's delve once again into our healthy and fulfilling marriage and ponder, "How did Jesus demonstrate love?"

THROUGHOUT HIS BRIEF time on earth, Jesus exemplified complete selflessness. His purpose wasn't rooted in self-fulfillment but in a higher calling. He imparted to His disciples in John 15:13, "Greater love hath no man than this, that a man lay down his life for his friends." Although they may not have grasped it fully then, Jesus was conveying that His love for them was profound enough to give up His life.

IMAGINE if I could express this depth of love to my wife. What if I could genuinely convey my willingness to devote myself entirely to her? We admire Secret Service officers who shield the President from bullets because they prioritize sacrificing themselves for another they deem more important.

WHAT IF, starting today, I decided to mirror that self-sacrificing love in my marriage? What if I declared, "This is no longer about what you can do for me! Our marriage isn't about my gains anymore. I'll stop fixating on what I receive and commit to giving my life for yours."

. . .

*Just Don't Feel Bad About The Problems
That You Have!*

JESUS PURPOSEFULLY LAID down His life. As we celebrate Easter this week, it's striking how misconceptions surround His crucifixion. Many portrayals depict a gentleman unfairly condemned and crucified by a hostile crowd. However, the Bible clarifies that neither the Jews who condemned Him nor the Romans who executed Him were ultimately responsible. Instead, Jesus made a deliberate choice out of love, declaring, "I love them enough to offer myself for them," willingly surrendering His life to redeem our eternal souls.

IN JOHN 10:18, Jesus affirms His agency in this sacrifice, stating,

> "No man taketh it from me, but I lay it down of myself. I have the power to lay it down, and I have the power to take it again."

HE TOLD HIS DISCIPLES, "No one will force me to the cross; I willingly choose to give myself."

GOD'S INTENTION and plan were to mend the broken relationship caused by sin. Whether we experience temporary or permanent rifts in relationships with parents, children, spouses, or friends, we all grapple with fractured connections. God created us with the deliberate purpose of fellowship with Him. It's astounding to think that initially, in the Garden of Eden, God walked alongside Adam and Eve in perfect harmony, devoid of conflict or discord. However, human disobedience disrupted this communion, introducing sin and rupturing our relationship with God.

ACKNOWLEDGING OUR SINFULNESS IS CHALLENGING; we prefer to deflect blame onto others. Some teachings attempt to soften this reality, urging us not to feel remorse for our actions. Yet, deep down, every individual must recognize their need for redemption and seek a Savior. It's tempting to shift responsibility, but this only amplifies selfishness, hindering our spiritual growth and relational harmony.

THE BLAME-DENIAL GAME we often play with God mirrors what happens in marriages. We can't simply ignore fights and issues, hoping they'll vanish. Our marital dynamics resemble a thermometer, where conflicts raise the "temperature" of frustration and anger. Each argument, even minor ones, incrementally heightens this level until it reaches a boiling point.

Our Marriage Relationship Is A Little Like a Thermometer

WE MAY TRY to act like nothing happened, but unresolved grudges and resentment keep our relational thermometer elevated. Small tussles compound over time until they strain our relationship to breaking. Avoiding admission of fault only exacerbates the situation, leading to inevitable explosions over trivial matters like burnt toast.

· · ·

ACKNOWLEDGING past problems is essential for restoring relationships. We must confess our mistakes rather than blaming external factors. Despite its unpopularity, recognizing our flaws is crucial for reconciliation with God and our loved ones.

WE ARE ALL FLAWED, requiring divine intervention. God sacrificed His Son not out of sorrow but as a joyful act to mend the fractured relationship between humanity and divinity. Jesus's ultimate act of love teaches us to lay down our lives for others, as articulated in 1 John 3:16.

> Hereby perceive we the love *of God*, because he laid down his life for us: and we ought to lay down *our* lives for the brethren.

PUBLIC APPEARANCES MAY SUGGEST perfect marriages, but private realities often differ. Our inability to mend relationships stems from our need for spiritual help. Without connecting with the ultimate Self-sacrificer, genuine change becomes elusive.

SELF-SACRIFICING LOVE, as demonstrated by Christ, involves restoring our relationship with God first, enabling us to repair relationships with others. Embracing Christ's love transforms bitterness and hurt into opportunities for healing and growth. It's through this transformative love that broken relationships find restoration and reconciliation.

WE NEED HELP. And that's why God chose to sacrifice His Son. I used to think that God felt nothing but sorrow and pain when the crucifixion happened. When His only Son died on a cross for the sins of the world, surely that caused God a great deal of hurt! But then I read in Isaiah 53 that

"it pleased the Lord to bruise Him"! (Is. 53:10)

THROUGH ALL THE horrors and suffering that Jesus went through to pay our debt, God the Father and God the Son experienced joy! They knew that they were making a way to restore the broken relationship between God and man. Jesus loved enough to love to give!

OUR CONCLUSION? We, too, should learn to lay down our lives for those we love. Maybe the reason we can't fix things at home is that we're in desperate need of help ourselves. Maybe the reason we can't sacrifice ourselves is that we're not connected to the great Self-sacrificer! For your marriage to be successful, it takes the efforts of three. Not just the work of a committed husband and a committed wife, but the power of God working to keep your relationship together. It's very hard for bitter people to love. It's hard for hurting people to love. But there is a solution! An answer to all the grief and hurt and mess you're going through. There is someone who can radically change your life! Self-sacrificing love boils down to our key verse, loving each other

like Christ loved the church and GAVE Himself for it.

HE SACRIFICED Himself for undeserving people. He wants to make sure that you have your relationship completely restored with Him first, and then you'll be able to start fixing your relationships with others, too!

Review

1. Selfishness Is An Inability To Deny Our Own Selves
2. At the core of most interpersonal conflicts is the presence of self-centeredness
3. The pursuit of personal comfort often becomes a dominating principle in our decision-making, leading us to make choices that prioritize our own ease and convenience, sometimes at the expense of those closest to us.
4. Nothing compares to the joy of being in a relationship where giving to each other is the guiding principle
5. It's tempting to shift responsibility, but this only amplifies selfishness, hindering our spiritual growth and relational harmony.

5

TILL DEATH DO US PART

In this chapter, we delve into the profound truths surrounding the enduring nature of certain commitments and the boundless love of our Heavenly Father. We will explore the concept of eternal security in Christ, understanding that once saved, we are forever cherished by God. We must embrace the reality of being eternally loved by a Holy God, whose power and love far surpass any challenges we may face.

It is crucial to grasp that God's love for us is everlasting, transcending time and circumstance. Despite our imperfections, failures, and doubts, His love remains steadfast and unwavering. Through His boundless love, we find assurance and comfort, knowing that our sins are forgiven and our souls are redeemed.

Furthermore, as we delve deeper into understanding God's love, we unlock the secrets to building healthy and fulfilling marriages. Even amidst marital struggles or relationship challenges, we can find comfort in God's infinite power to mend and restore. His desire is for us to experience joy and fulfillment in our relationships, both now and in the days to come.

ULTIMATELY, God's love serves as a beacon of hope and inspiration, demonstrating the depth of His compassion and grace. As we learn to emulate His love in our relationships, we discover the transformative power of love that transcends all obstacles. Indeed, the God we serve is infinitely great, showering us with His enduring love and guidance every step of the way.

LEST WE FORGET, let's look at our theme verse again,

> *Husbands, **love** your wives, even as Christ also **loved** the church, and **gave** himself for it; Ephesians 5:25.*

THE FOUNDATION of all the teachings in this book rests upon a pivotal verse that sparked a profound realization in my life. I vividly recall the moment when, as a missionary in Peru, I delved deeper into this verse while studying my Bible in Spanish. Despite having read it numerous times before, the richness of its meaning unfolded in a new and impactful way through the Spanish wording.

THE VERSE INSTRUCTS husbands to love their wives "asi como" Christ loved the church, which can be translated as "just like" or "in the same way." This revelation struck me like a bolt of lightning – if I were to love my wife and children in the same sacrificial and selfless manner that Jesus loves me, I am certain that our home would overflow with joy and harmony.

· · ·

THIS PROFOUND TRUTH underscores the transformative power of love modeled after Christ's own love for His church. It challenges us to embody His unconditional love, forgiveness, and grace in our relationships, particularly within the sanctity of our marriage. As we embrace this divine standard of love, we unlock the potential for a home filled with happiness, peace, and lasting fulfillment.

HAVE you ever found yourself feeling bored while reading your Bible? It's not uncommon to experience a sense of monotony when encountering familiar passages, where the words can seem like the same old routine that we've read and heard countless times before. However, if we're not mindful, we may overlook the profound messages that God is conveying to us through these words. We risk missing out on the intimate and personal communication that God desires to have with each of us. Sadly, this is often the case with passages like the one we're about to explore – passages that hold immense potential for healing and transformation, yet are frequently overlooked or skimmed through.

A Healthy and Fulfilling Marriage Vows to Last
"Till Death Do Us Part!"

THROUGHOUT OUR JOURNEY, we've explored the multifaceted love of Christ and gleaned valuable relationship principles from His example. But there's more to discover about how He loved the church.

REFLECTING on my own marriage to Betty on August 18, 1973, I recall uttering the familiar vows that echo through many weddings: "til death do us part." However, over the years, I've come to realize that these words can sometimes ring hollow, as marriages face challenges that test their endurance. Yet, when God makes a promise to stand by you, there's an unwavering certainty that He will indeed fulfill His word, no matter what trials may come.

NO MATTER what your past may entail, there's a steadfast truth you can rely on – God is always ready to extend His forgiveness and welcome you into His loving family! If you haven't yet embarked on a restored relationship with God, today is the perfect opportunity to do so. However, it's crucial to understand that once you receive His forgiveness, it's not a temporary offer; it's an enduring promise that spans into your future as well.

YOUR PAST, no matter how significant, loses its grip when confronted with God's boundless mercy. Equally reassuring is the fact that nothing in your future, no matter how daunting, can ever sever the unbreakable bond between you and the love of God. In essence, God's promise to you surpasses any vow you may have made on your wedding day – He guarantees that not even death itself can separate you from His loving presence.

GOD DESIRES for you to find security and peace in the knowledge that His love for you knows no bounds. It's a love that transcends time, circumstances, and even mortality, offering you the assurance of unconditional and eternal acceptance in His embrace.

It's Your Decision

As we dig into the comparison of Christ's love with our own, let's ponder the profound aspect of duration. How long does God plan on loving us?

.   .   .

IF YOU'RE A PARENT, you understand firsthand that parenting inevitably comes with its share of challenges as your children grow. The once easily manageable little ones suddenly become more independent, testing boundaries and asserting their own will. It's a familiar journey for many parents; the anticipation of their children reaching an age where they listen and obey seems to linger indefinitely. Betty and I have personally experienced this waiting game over many years and sometimes it seems that our children never quite reach that stage!

HOWEVER, I want to draw your attention to a remarkable decision that Christ made in His love for us, a decision that surpasses our human understanding. Despite our unruliness and shortcomings, which far exceed any challenges we face as parents, Christ made a resolute choice rooted in love. We find this profound truth echoed in Jeremiah 31:3, where God declares,

"I have loved thee with an everlasting love."

TAKE a moment to let that sink in – God's love for us is not bound by time or circumstance; it is eternal, enduring, and unchanging. It's a truth worth highlighting in your Bible, a reminder of the incredible depth of His love that remains constant throughout our journey.

PERHAPS WHEN YOU CONTEMPLATE SALVATION, doubts and insecurities creep in. You might think, "I desire to be saved and transformed by God, but I'm not sure I can handle it. I doubt my ability to live up to God's expectations and be the person He wants me to be." Here's the beautiful truth you need to grasp – God's everlasting love for you transcends your past failures, current struggles, and uncertainties about the future. It's a love that accepts you as you are, embraces you in your imperfections, and promises to walk with you through every season of life.

WHEN YOU ENCOUNTER a love like that – a love that sees beyond externalities and embraces you wholeheartedly – you know you've discovered something truly extraordinary and life-changing.

INDEED, the duration of God's love surpasses any contractual terms – it is an eternal, boundless love. There's no prenuptial contract for you to sign when God extends His saving grace to you. Unlike what religion sometimes portrays, salvation is not a transactional agreement where you must meet certain conditions to receive God's love and forgiveness. God's love is not contingent on your performance or adherence to a set of rules. He didn't lay out a list of demands, saying, "I'll love you and send my Son to die for you only if you meet these conditions." Christianity should never be reduced to a contract-based love – a conditional love that operates on an "either do this or else" premise.

A Contract Is A Legal Agreement Based on DISTRUST.

CONSIDER THIS: a contract is essentially a legal agreement born out of mutual distrust, where both parties seek to protect their own interests and rights. However, our marriages and certainly our salvation are not meant to be based on such contractual terms. A contract brings forth existence due to skepticism and the desire to safeguard oneself.

.   .   .

DURING MY TIME IN PERU, I often found myself navigating through legal contracts, acting as a mediator for fellow expatriates who needed assistance with rental paperwork. The legal intricacies were already overwhelming, especially in another language. I vividly remember my early days in Peru, where suspicion and caution clouded my judgment, causing me to scrutinize every contract detail meticulously.

ONE PARTICULAR INSTANCE STANDS OUT, where I insisted on reading through a rental contract despite pressure to quickly sign it. To my surprise, I discovered a hidden clause that would have been detrimental to me financially. This experience reinforced the idea that contracts are often laden with clauses and provisions designed to protect one party's interests, highlighting the inherent distrust that underpins contractual agreements.

IN MANY OF OUR RELATIONSHIPS, there's an unspoken "IF" that governs our interactions – "I'll be your friend IF you do this for me." While there may not be formal contracts, these relational dynamics operate similarly, driven by a sense of self-preservation and caution. Contracts, in essence, reflect our innate distrust of human nature and our inclination to shield ourselves from potential harm or exploitation.

IN CONTRAST, God's love defies contractual norms. It is unconditional, unchanging, and everlasting. It transcends human limitations and biases, offering a love that is pure, genuine, and unwavering. There's no need for contracts or conditions in God's love – it simply exists, encompassing us in its embrace without reservation or hesitation.

. . .

THE BIBLE INTRODUCES a profound shift in the dynamics of relationships by presenting a covenant instead of a contract. Unlike a contract, which is rooted in doubt and self-protection, a covenant is built upon trust, faith, love, loyalty, and confidence. Understanding this distinction is crucial, as it can mean the difference between a thriving, life-giving relationship and one fraught with misunderstandings and limitations.

> Yet ye say, Wherefore? Because the Lord hath been witness between thee and the wife of thy youth, Against whom thou hast dealt treacherously: Yet *is* **she thy companion, and the wife of thy covenant.** Malachi 2:14.

IN MALACHI 2:14, the Bible describes the relationship between a husband and wife as a covenant: "yet is she thy companion, and the wife of thy covenant." When Betty and I embarked on our marital journey, we were young and inexperienced, unaware of the need for a formal contract. However, the Bible beautifully captures the essence of our commitment as "the wife of my covenant" – a bond grounded in unconditional love and mutual trust.

Unlike a Contract, A Covenant Is Based on TRUST.

GOD'S SAVING love operates within the framework of a covenant, not a contract. The narrative of salvation revolves around God's unwavering decision to love us unconditionally, irrespective of our past, present, or future. He extends His love as a gift, without demanding that we earn it through our actions or merits.

.   .   .

EPHESIANS 2:8-9 articulates this truth succinctly:

"For by grace are ye saved through faith; and that not of yourselves: it is the gift of God: not of works, lest any man should boast."

GOD DIDN'T SET forth conditions for our salvation, expecting us to measure up or prove our worthiness. Instead, He demonstrated His boundless love by offering His Son as a gift, a sacrifice beyond anything we could ever deserve or earn.

For the wages of sin *is* death; but the gift of God *is* eternal life through Jesus Christ our Lord. Romans 6:23.

IN MY RELATIONSHIPS with my children and wife, I strive to emulate this covenantal love – a love that chooses to extend grace and forgiveness even when it's undeserved. It's about honoring the covenant that exists between us, just as God honored His covenant with us through Christ's sacrifice. Romans 6:23 beautifully encapsulates this reality, reminding us that while we were deserving of death, God bestowed upon us the gift of eternal life out of His unconditional love.

IN ESSENCE, understanding the difference between a covenant and a contract reshapes our perspective on relationships, emphasizing the power of unconditional love, grace, and the gift of salvation offered to us by God.

And I **give** unto them eternal life; and they shall never perish, neither shall any *man* **pluck** them out of my hand.

John 10:28.

IN JOHN 10:28, Jesus provided His disciples with tangible proof of the covenant established between Him and His children. He assured us that we are securely held in His protective hand, and no force in the universe is potent enough to snatch us away from His grasp. Let's fully embrace the assurance of Christ's words and witness the unfailing nature of this covenant! Let's wholeheartedly believe God's declaration that salvation is an unconditional covenant – a promise that stands firm regardless of circumstances. Just as Jesus assured His disciples then, He affirms to us today: "I have made the decision, and so has My Father; we are united, and the Holy Trinity is in agreement that nothing will ever separate us again!"

NOW, how does this profound truth relate to my marriage? It's fundamentally about making a decision on my part. I must actively choose to uphold the covenant I entered into with my wife on the day of our marriage. I must commit myself to stand by her side through thick and thin, unwavering in my dedication to honor the vows I made. Challenges may arise along the way, but I am determined not only to fulfill my responsibilities but also to uphold the sanctity of our covenant. This critical decision to honor our marriage covenant is something that each of us must embrace and uphold in our relationships.

ULTIMATELY, just as God's covenant with us is unbreakable and everlasting, so too should our commitment to our marital covenant be unwavering and enduring. It's about embodying the same level of steadfastness and dedication that God demonstrates in His covenant with us, ensuring that our relationships thrive on the foundation of trust, love, and unwavering commitment.

The Vow

You Don't Have To Live UNSECURE!

The message of covenant love is profoundly liberating – it frees us from insecurity and doubt. We no longer need to question whether God accepts us or loves us because He has already chosen to love and forgive us unconditionally. This assurance extends beyond our ability to make covenant-honoring decisions in our earthly relationships; God has already made the ultimate decision in His relationship with us. He has freely offered salvation, a gift that goes against our prideful nature as we often seek to earn or own things rather than receive them as gifts. Salvation is something we could never achieve on our own due to our weaknesses and helplessness, yet God's love surpasses all barriers.

GOD DOESN'T SPEAK of His covenant in uncertain terms or future tense. Consider His words in John 5:24:

> "He that heareth My word, and believeth on Him that sent Me, hath everlasting life, and shall not come into condemnation, but is passed from death unto life."

JESUS UNEQUIVOCALLY STATES that whoever hears His words and
believes in Him already possesses eternal life. There's no ambiguity –
it's a present reality, not a distant hope or possibility.

So, what happens if, after being saved, we stumble or make mistakes
years down the line? Does God retract the life He promised? Abso-
lutely not. That wouldn't be everlasting life; it would be temporary
and conditional. God's love is not conditional on our behavior or
actions; it is an enduring, everlasting love that transcends our failures
and shortcomings. How comforting it is to know that we have a God
whose love is eternal, a love that lasts forever and ever.

LET'S delve deeper into the next phrase of the verse: "Shall not come
into condemnation." This statement carries immense weight – it
unequivocally declares that condemnation is simply not on the table.
Once you've transitioned from death to life in God's realm, there's no
going back. In His divine economy, there are no distinctions based on
external factors like race, nationality, or social status. Instead, there
are only two fundamental categories: life and death, saved and lost,
known by God and unknown. Once you find yourself in the "life"
column, there's no possibility of facing the "condemnation" reserved
for the "death" column.

When Things Get Rough,
Remind Yourself of Your Promise!

GOD HAS MADE a solemn vow to you: "You hear, you believe, you
have." It's not a promise for the future; it's a present reality that
encompasses everything you need and lasts for eternity.

. . .

CONSIDER the vows exchanged in marriage ceremonies. Amidst the nervousness and excitement, it's easy to recite them without fully grasping their significance. As someone who officiates weddings, I've witnessed countless couples uttering the familiar words: "in sickness or in health, for richer or for poorer, for better or for worse 'til death do us part." These vows represent a profound commitment where two individuals pledge to stand by each other's side through every circumstance, pledging their lives and declaring that nothing but death itself can sever their bond.

WHEN CHALLENGES ARISE in your marriage, remember the solemn promise you made. Remind yourself that you're bound by a vow, a commitment that requires you to seek reconciliation and work through difficulties. Upholding this commitment is key to navigating marital challenges successfully. It's about embracing the responsibility and duty inherent in your vow, ensuring that your actions align with the promises you've made. If you approach marriage with a mindset of steadfast commitment and unwavering dedication, you're more likely to find solutions and weather storms together. Conversely, if you view marriage with a casual "wait and see" attitude, you may find that challenges become insurmountable.

IN OVER 50 years of marriage, Betty and I have enjoyed a harmonious relationship without any major conflicts (except for the occasional skirmish I've mentioned). However, there was a time early in our marriage when I was working on staff at a church in Alabama. We lived in a small apartment above a garage with our first baby. One day, I returned home after spending several hours in air-conditioned comfort with the pastor, while Betty was struggling with a bout of diarrhea. The apartment was chaotic, with moving boxes every-where, and our baby was wailing. Instead of offering comfort or assistance, my initial reaction was to question Betty about her activities during the day, which was clearly not the right approach.

LOOKING BACK, I realize I was only 21 and didn't always know the best way to communicate with my wife. Of course, even at 70 and over, I still make mistakes. My attempts to communicate further only escalated the situation, leading to a heated exchange of words and me storming out, threatening to leave until I cooled off. However, my exit was thwarted when Betty hurled a metal sport whistle at me with surprising accuracy, a moment that later added humor to the tense situation.

We Fixed It Simply Because We HAD to!

AFTER SOME TIME REFLECTING OUTSIDE, I realized the folly of my actions and returned home to make amends with my wife. We apologized to each other and worked through our differences, reaffirming our commitment to each other and our marriage vows. This experience taught me the importance of honoring our vow to love each other for life, especially during challenging times when conflicts arise.

MARRIAGE IS NOT ALWAYS smooth sailing; conflicts and disagreements are inevitable. However, it's crucial to remember our commitment and follow the example of Christ in our relationships. Jesus didn't place conditions on His love or make His sacrifice contingent on our obedience. Instead, He demonstrated unconditional love and promised eternal companionship.

· · ·

IF YOU'RE FACING challenges in your marriage, remember your vows and commit to lifelong companionship. Jesus assures us of His presence and support until the end, regardless of our imperfections or struggles. Keeping our vows and offering unconditional love to our spouses can lead to remarkable transformations and strengthen our marriages.

Working through the problem

Salvation with God isn't a half-hearted arrangement. To grasp the essence of Christ's love, we must understand this fundamental aspect. When God loves, He sees us in our brokenness and loves us unconditionally. Even when we stumble again, His love remains unwavering. It was Jesus who initiated this love, not us. He gave everything required to sustain the relationship—there were no conditions or percentages left for us to fulfill.

CONSIDER EPHESIANS 5, often referred to as the healthy and fulfilling marriage chapter, which elaborates on God's role in salvation:

- He is the Savior of the body (v.23).
- He loved the church (v.25).
- He gave Himself for the church (v.25).
- He sanctifies and cleanses it (v.26).
- He will gloriously present it to Himself (v.27).

CLEARLY, salvation is not a 50-50 deal but a complete work of God's love. When Jesus sacrificed Himself on the cross, He declared, "It is finished," signifying the full payment for our salvation. Our failures and shortcomings didn't deter Him; He willingly bore the entire cost, leaving no room for doubt or insecurity.

. . .

She's My Wife, And I'll Buy Her Back!

THIS PRINCIPLE of loving in spite of failure is exemplified in the book of Hosea. The prophet Hosea married Gomer, a known prostitute, to illustrate how God loves and saves us not based on our merits but our need for His grace. Despite Gomer's repeated unfaithfulness and sinful lifestyle, Hosea continued to love her unconditionally. Even when Gomer faced public humiliation and was put up for sale as a slave, Hosea stepped forward and bought her back, demonstrating his enduring love.

THIS STORY TEACHES us that no matter how broken or undeserving we feel, God's love remains constant. Whether you're seeking salvation or struggling after being saved, God's forgiveness and love are always available. You can experience the wonder of God's unconditional love and find strength to navigate through life's challenges together.

SO, if you're hurting or lost, remember Gomer's story. God stands ready to forgive, redeem, and love you despite your failures. Rest assured in His covenant love, knowing that He will always stand by you, ready to accept and love you until the end.

6

BUILDING DREAM RELATIONSHIPS

S o far, we've drilled into what we should avoid in relationships. Perhaps now you're curious about what steps are needed to construct a new home after the old one has been dismantled. That's precisely what we'll explore next: building a healthy and fulfilling marriage, a concept I believe resonates with all of us deeply. To achieve this, we must adopt a fresh perspective on family relationships, shedding old notions and embracing the model provided by God:

"Husbands, love your wives, **even as** Christ also loved the church and gave Himself for it; that He might sanctify and cleanse it with the washing of water by the word, that He might present it to Himself a glorious church, not having spot, or wrinkle, or any such thing; but that it should be holy and without blemish." Ephesians 5:25-27

THIS INDEED PAINTS a vivid picture of the ultimate healthy and fulfilling marriage relationship! It's a concept that sparks excitement and contemplation. When Jesus extended His love to us, desiring to draw us closer into a relationship with Him, He demonstrated a constructive love, even though He had every reason to turn to a destructive approach. Instead of condemning us for our failures and sinful nature, He chose to uplift us, to "edify" us, and build us up. He could have easily distanced Himself from us, refusing to engage with our issues and challenges. However, He made the deliberate choice to foster a new and transformative relationship with us.

Will You Use Your Authority To Be Constructive or Destructive?

RECOGNIZING THIS PERSPECTIVE, I realize that my approach to relationships must reflect this constructive love. Just as Jesus embarked on a monumental task to initiate a love relationship with sinful humanity, I must also undertake a significant construction project in my relationships, particularly with my family. It's essential to reject the notion of quick fixes and commit to the long-term effort required for building a strong and loving home environment. This involves developing detailed plans and making necessary preparations for the construction project of love within my home.

VERSE 27 BEAUTIFULLY illustrates how Jesus will one day present the church to Himself as a completed project, showcasing the culmination of His invested work and sacrifices. Just as He will receive the glorious finished product of His efforts, committing to building healthy and fulfilling marriage relationships can also lead to enjoying the benefits of living in a healthy and fulfilling marriage.

For though I should boast somewhat more of our authority, which the Lord hath **given** us for edification, and not for your destruction, I should not be **ashamed**: 2 Corinthians 10:8.

IN II CORINTHIANS 10:8, Paul emphasizes that the authority he possesses, given by the Lord for edification and not destruction, serves a specific purpose. He could boast about his authority as a man of God, but he clarifies that its purpose is solely for edification— the uplifting and improvement of others.

LOVE RELATIONSHIPS inherently come with significant authority. Your influence and sway over the people in your home are considerable, even if it may not always feel that way. During dating, much of your actions were likely influenced by the wishes and desires of your loved one. Similarly, in marriage and family life, your handling of authority significantly impacts the daily atmosphere and well-being of your household.

REFLECTING ON THIS AUTHORITY, akin to what the Apostle Paul spoke about, raises a crucial question: how will you wield it? Will you use it constructively or destructively? Constructive love aims to build up others, initiating improvement projects that eventually lead to a healthy and fulfilling marriage. On the contrary, destructive love tears down loved ones, resulting in shattered home relationships. The choice between constructive and destructive love profoundly shapes the harmony and happiness within your home.

HERE ARE four simple truths about the principle of constructive love and its power to build a healthy and fulfilling marriage:

The Cost of a Healthy and Fulfilling Marriage

What does it cost to have contrastive love?

CONSTRUCTIVE LOVE, much like any construction project, often ends up costing more than initially anticipated. Unexpected expenses tend to arise at the worst times, leading to doubts and second-guessing. This phenomenon is common in home projects; just when you commit to building a healthy and fulfilling marriage, challenges surface, making you question the worth of your efforts.

Though the Cost of the Project Adds Up,
It's Worth the Cost!

CONSIDER WEDDINGS—A time of beauty and joy, but the real journey starts afterward. The myth of "two can live as cheap as one" quickly dispels, revealing the true costs of marriage. Real relationships always come with a price tag.

REFLECTING ON JESUS' example, His constructive love came at a great cost. He came to give abundant life but had to sacrifice His life on the cross to fulfill that purpose. Likewise, relationships demand sacrifices and investments.

PERHAPS YOUR MARRIAGE FACES CHALLENGES, and you desire a healthy and fulfilling marriage relationship. Understand that it's achievable but comes at a substantial cost. Salvation, though free, wasn't cheap for God—it cost Him His Son's life and countless efforts from the Holy Spirit.

Look not every man **on** his own things, but every man also **on** the things of others. Philippians 2:4.

As HUMANS, we often focus on our problems, but the Bible urges us to consider others' needs. Christ exemplified this selflessness by giving His life for us, despite His divine position and comfort in heaven. His sacrifice teaches us the essence of love that considers others above oneself.

The Belief of a Healthy and Fulfilling Marriage Relationship

In 1 Corinthians 13, often dubbed the "love chapter," love is described as believing all things, hoping all things, and enduring all things. Real love holds a belief that anything is possible and anticipates great outcomes.

CONSTRUCTIVE LOVE inherently believes in the potential of the loved one. It perceives them not just as they are but envisions the greatness they can achieve.

THERE'S a story about an African chief seeking a bride. Despite the villagers showcasing their daughters adorned in their best, the chief chose the least attractive girl, believing in her hidden beauty. He paid a substantial price for her, and years later, she emerged as a stunning queen. The chief's belief transformed her.

. . .

SIMILARLY, our families may lack a healthy and fulfilling marriage relationships because we fail to believe in our partners' potential. As a spouse or parent, your belief can shape their destiny significantly. What you speak over them influences their future. If you speak negativity, that's what they may become. Therefore, infuse them with a sense of destiny and belief.

REFLECTING on the biblical story of Gideon, God saw potential in him when he saw himself as insignificant. God's belief in Gideon led to his transformation into a mighty leader.

BETTY ONCE SAID to me during our church's humble beginnings, "When I see you today behind that box, I know that one day you'll stand in big places behind big pulpits and preach to big crowds. God's going to give you that one day." Her belief in my potential kept me going during challenging times.

IN YOUR RELATIONSHIPS, embrace constructive love by believing in the greatness within your loved ones, even when others don't see it. Expect remarkable things from them and speak words of affirmation and encouragement that nurture their growth and potential. This belief in them can pave the way for healthy and fulfilling marriage relationships to flourish.

YEARS LATER, Betty and I found ourselves seated on a platform in Peru, with 150 people behind us and a vast crowd of 1,500 people in front of us. In those moments, I could sense what Betty was thinking. She had seen me standing with a pulpit when all I had was a makeshift box. She had envisioned me leading a church when we only had an old gift shop. She had believed in me speaking to a large crowd when we started with just a few individuals.

. . .

Do you believe in your partner? Do you express that unwavering belief? What about your children? Do you see their current challenges as defining them, or do you envision the incredible individuals they can become? Genuine belief in your family is crucial if you want to cultivate a healthy and fulfilling marriage relationship. Believe in their potential, just as God believes in yours. He showed His belief by sending His Son to redeem you, recognizing the immense value in your life and the incredible potential for greatness.

On the flip side, there are things you should never believe. Don't assume intentionality in offenses or doubt their love. Refuse to entertain accusations or voices of doubt.

Real love believes in the strength of the relationship. Do your loved ones know that you believe in them? Start expressing your belief today!

The Power of Words in a healthy and fulfilling marriage Relationships

Paul emphasized the significance of our words in building a healthy and fulfilling marriage relationships: "Let no corrupt communication proceed out of your mouth, but that which is good to the use of edifying, that it may minister grace unto the hearers" (Ephesians 4:29). Here, "corrupt communication" refers to destructive words rather than explicit language. Have you considered the impact of your words? They possess the power to uplift or tear down.

. . .

PAUL URGED the church to use words that edify and bring grace to others—a personal gift we offer to our family through communication.

REFLECT on your recent interactions with your spouse. Were they filled with criticism and blame, or did they express admiration and appreciation? Constructive love ensures that our words only serve to uplift and strengthen one another.

YEARS AGO, a captivating experiment was conducted by Harvard professor Robert Rosenthal. They gathered a group of teachers from a particular county and informed them, "You are the top educators in the county! You are exceptional, and we want to include you in an experiment. For one year, you'll have the best students in the county." Delighted by this recognition, the teachers eagerly agreed. Simultaneously, they gathered the students and told them, "You are the top students in the county, and you'll have the best teachers for one year."

THE ASTONISHING OUTCOME? These students performed 30%-40% better than others. It was revealed later that both the teachers and the students were randomly selected, but the belief in their greatness fueled their success. This experiment underscores the power of words in building people up.

EXPRESSING admiration and respect is vital. Wives, your husbands thrive on admiration and respect, even if they don't always admit it. Men, in general, need affirmation and appreciation, so don't hesitate to speak well of them to others. This positive reinforcement can have a profound impact.

. . .

SOME OF US struggle to express constructive sentiments. I recall an incident from my early missionary days in Mexico. I attempted to express appreciation to a Christian man named Alberto by saying, "I love you." He was taken aback and suggested saying, "I love you in Christ," due to cultural differences.

SIMILARLY, as fathers, we may find it challenging to express love, especially to our sons as they grow older. Yet, it's crucial to maintain this expression of love. I remember the significance of hearing my father speak highly of me without knowing I was listening. Such unexpected affirmations can mean the world to our loved ones.

IN CONCLUSION, never underestimate the impact of positive words. They have the power to uplift, inspire, and strengthen relationships in profound ways. Express love and admiration freely, even if it feels uncomfortable at times. It can create lasting bonds and build a healthy and fulfilling marriage relationships.

BE cautious about using reverse psychology, negative hints, or underhanded comments. These tactics may seem like shortcuts to getting what we want, but they often cause significant harm. I've personally fallen into the trap of saying the opposite of what I meant, using veiled words that hurt my family as much as direct insults would have. This is especially common among men who may prefer toughness over sweetness. Making remarks about weight, appearance, or personal hygiene, even in jest, can inflict deep pain. We sometimes deceive ourselves into thinking we're addressing issues with our words, but destructive words only cause hurt; they never build.

. . .

HERE'S a crucial piece of advice regarding words in a healthy and fulfilling marriage relationship: ensure your words are not just empty promises. You can only hide your true feelings behind words for so long before your true self emerges. The Bible speaks about this in 1 Peter 3:1, advising wives with unbelieving husbands that their actions can win them over without uttering a word. The lifestyle and conduct of a believing spouse carry more weight than mere words.

TO BE FRANK, talk is inexpensive. Believing in someone and expressing it genuinely through words are distinct actions. Your actions and lifestyle are more potent indicators of your beliefs than what you say. Simply saying "I love you" multiple times won't instantly dissolve long-standing issues in your relationship. It takes time and consistent effort to rebuild trust and mend broken bonds. Your spouse may remain skeptical until they see consistent changes in your behavior.

IF you genuinely want to mend things at home, your actions will speak louder than words. It's natural for things to feel more challenging even after you start saying the right things; this could be because trust takes time to rebuild. Don't give up on communicating positivity and love constructively. Keep showing through your actions that you're committed to making things right.

The Love in a Healthy and Fulfilling Marriage Relationship

John's contemplation of God's love for him led him to exclaim,

"Behold, what manner of love the Father hath bestowed upon us, that we should be called the sons of God" I John 3:1

HIS WORDS RESONATE with joyful astonishment, capturing the overwhelming nature of God's love. It's a love that accepts us just as we are, a hallmark of healthy and fulfilling marriage relationships that say, "I am content with you as you are right now."

IT'S common to feel like we'll never quite measure up. We live in a world where satisfaction can feel elusive. A child brings home a good grade, and we wonder why it wasn't better. They achieve excellence, and we push for perfection. The cycle of expectation can seem never-ending, especially in our closest relationships.

HOWEVER, God's love is different. It's unconditional and unchanging. We don't have to earn it or meet certain standards. God simply loves us for who we are. Imagine loving your spouse or family member with that same kind of unconditional acceptance, appreciating them just as they are today.

THERE'S humor and truth in Betty's response about not having the time to train another spouse—it took thirty years to get the current one right! Many couples struggle with trying to mold each other into their ideal image. But constructive love says, "I love you just as you are, without conditions or expectations."

IN MY EXPERIENCES IN PERU, I've seen parents oblivious to their children's mischiefs until someone points them out. It's a reminder that we often notice faults more than virtues. However, love covers a multitude of sins. In a healthy and fulfilling marriage relationship, both partners choose to love in a way that forgives and overlooks mistakes.

·   ·   ·

BUILDING a healthy and fulfilling marriage relationship involves accepting the cost, believing in each other, speaking positively, and loving constructively. Remember, your relationship isn't just about the two of you; it also includes a relationship with God. As you seek to love and obey Him, your love for each other will deepen and grow sweeter, creating the ultimate healthy and fulfilling marriage home.

A LOVE OF GRACE

At this juncture, we've witnessed five amazing aspects of Christ's love for His church, each serving as a guiding principle on our journey to constructing our healthy and fulfilling marriage. If you're still engaged with this book, it's because you're among a large community of couples genuinely seeking enduring marriages in an era where such stability is rare. Our world is fraught with separations, divorces, estrangements, conflicts, and pain, often considered the norm. Yet, we continue to envision resilient, joyful marriages that serve as sanctuaries for our families. I trust that by now, you share my belief that this vision is not just a fantasy but a tangible reality within your grasp—for you and your loved ones.

TERRIBLE EVENTS MIGHT HAVE OCCURRED in your marriage by now. However, dwelling on the past will only cast shadows on our future. Instead of fixating on past issues, embracing the teachings of the Bible regarding Christ's love can pave the way for resolving challenges and fostering a happier marriage in the days ahead.

. . .

Let's revisit our core concept once again: the foundation of our healthy and fulfilling marriage lies in living out the love of Christ for us, which in turn shapes our love for our families. By loving our families in the same way Christ loved the church, our marriages naturally become joyful sanctuaries! Each of the five principles we've extracted from His immense love stems from this central idea: "even as Christ." As I envision my healthy and fulfilling marriage, I seek a flawless model of love and compassion. I seek guidance on how to cherish my wife, children, and others in my life. This guidance is found in the example of Jesus Christ – there is simply no greater love than the love God bestows upon us!

> Husbands, **love** your wives, even as Christ also **loved** the church, and **gave** himself for it; Ephesians 5:25.

This ultimate truth regarding the love of Christ is particularly dear to me! Even if the other principles didn't exist or hadn't impacted me, this one is essential for my relationship with God to flourish. This principle, known as "a love of grace," is what ensures that I am loved by God even when I am undeserving!

What does it truly mean to love with grace?

It's the steadfast commitment to love, even when marriage throws challenges our way that seem insurmountable. There are moments when the other principles we've discussed may not immediately yield results. It's during these trying times that a love filled with grace becomes the cornerstone of a successful home.

You might initially think, "Our marriage could never reach that breaking point. We've had our ups and downs, but we'll never face such difficulties." While I won't dispute your optimism, the reality is that many couples find themselves at this juncture more often than expected. It's at this juncture that understanding and embodying a love of grace becomes crucial.

How did Christ demonstrate His love for the church? He loved us even when we were undeserving. And how does Christ continue to love me despite my daily shortcomings? It's because He embodies grace-filled love—a love that extends to us even when we feel we least deserve it.

Grace love is unconditional and unmerited. It's a love that Jesus demonstrated when He saved me, despite my utter lack of deserving it. In contrast to what some religious teachings may imply, God's love doesn't wait for us to be ready or worthy. His love says, "I love you regardless of your flaws and shortcomings."

This type of love is essential because, let's face it, none of us are perfect. We all have moments where we fall short, whether in our roles as spouses, parents, or children. Have you ever experienced those challenging times in marriage when it seemed like your partner's mood would never improve? Or those moments as a parent when your child's behavior tested your patience beyond measure?

Every family encounters obstacles and difficulties. There are days when our children are delightful, and then there are moments when they push us to our limits. The reality is that life brings its share of challenges, and that's when grace love becomes paramount.

As it is written, There is none righteous, no, not one: 11 There is none
that understandeth, there is none that seeketh after God. 12 They are
all gone out of the way, they are together become unprofitable; there
is none that doeth good, no, not one. Romans 3:10–12.

EVEN WHEN OUR loved ones aren't at their best, grace love compels us
to love them anyway. Jesus exemplified this kind of love by choosing
to love us despite our flaws and imperfections. Romans 3:10-12 paints
a stark picture of humanity's shortcomings, highlighting that no one
is righteous or deserving on their own.

DESPITE THESE ABSOLUTES, God's grace love extends to each one of us.
It's a love that perseveres through the toughest times and sees beyond
our faults. Just as we receive grace from God, we're called to extend
that same grace love to our families, especially when they need it
most.

THE SURVEY RESULTS ARE IN, and it's unanimous across the human
race: none of us are perfect. While some may be morally upright,
kind-hearted, or generally good, perfection eludes us all. This reality
hits home when we read in Romans 3:23 that

"all have sinned and come short of the glory of God,"

UNDERSCORING our collective inability to meet God's impeccable
standard, no matter how hard we try.

. . .

THE CRUX of the matter is that we cannot attain goodness or earn God's favor through our efforts alone. No amount of striving or self-improvement can bridge the gap between our imperfection and God's perfection. We can't simply rely on our own merits to please God or expect Him to overlook our wrongdoings. A mere majority of good deeds or an almost-perfect record falls short in God's eyes—we've all fallen short of His ideal and rely entirely on His grace love for redemption.

HAVE you ever pondered when God's love begins or ends for you? It's not contingent on when you stop engaging in certain behaviors or start living a certain way. His love extends to you even in the depths of your worst sins. In fact, His sacrificial act on the cross encompassed all your past, present, and future transgressions—He loved you precisely at your lowest point when you might have thought you were unlovable.

SO, how does this relate to our families? It's the essence of everything! If we're called to love like Christ, then we must embody grace love—a love that extends to our loved ones on their darkest days, even when they least deserve it. We must be ready to love them through their faults and shortcomings, just as God loves us unconditionally despite our failings.

IN THE GRAND scheme of things, there's no checklist of good deeds that can justify us before God or mend our broken relationship with Him. It's not about what we do; it's about recognizing our need for His grace love and embracing it fully.

THERE ARE no rigid rules to follow when it comes to grace love. It's not a matter of transitioning from being "messed up" to suddenly "fixed up" by adhering to a checklist. Let me share an anecdote to illustrate this point.

UPON JOINING MY LOCAL YMCA, I was eager to get into shape. The trainer gave me a personalized exercise program to achieve my fitness goals, complete with machines that tracked my progress and applauded my efforts. However, despite the positive reinforcement, I soon found myself neglecting the gym altogether.

UNLIKE PHYSICAL FITNESS, spiritual fitness doesn't operate on a quantifiable scale of push-ups and sit-ups. You can't approach God like a doctor and ask for a prescribed regimen to earn His favor. The truth is, our efforts to make things right with God fall short—it's an impossible task on our own.

GRACE LOVE, the very love that saves us, is bestowed upon us without any merit on our part. God saw me in my brokenness before my salvation—a mess of imperfections that were symptoms of a deeper spiritual struggle.

ALLOW me to share a childhood memory that reflects my early missteps. In second grade, I resorted to copying a classmate's test answers, only to be betrayed by a teacher who orchestrated my fail-ure. This incident marked the beginning of my "criminal" endeavors, including petty theft from a local store.

REFLECTING on these moments from my past, I recognize the depths of God's love. Despite my flaws and wrongdoings, He loved me unconditionally. This love extends to our relationships as well, espe-cially during times when our loved ones may not be at their best.

. . .

PERHAPS YOU'VE EXPERIENCED moments when your partner or family members were less than lovable, or when your contributions seemed one-sided. In my own marriage, I've often been at fault. However, a strong relationship requires a mindset of giving rather than taking.

WHEN JESUS CAME into my life, I had nothing to offer Him except my brokenness. I was far from deserving, yet He showed me grace love. Sharing these personal stories isn't to glorify wrongdoing but to highlight the transformative power of grace.

IN HIGH SCHOOL, I made regrettable choices, showcasing a darker side of my character. These actions were driven by selfishness and a lack of moral compass. It's humbling to admit these past mistakes, knowing that grace love was extended to me despite my shortcomings.

THE ESSENCE of grace love is that it meets us where we are, irrespective of our failings or past sins. It's a love that doesn't wait for us to become worthy but embraces us in our brokenness and offers redemption.

MANY OF US readily acknowledge our past mistakes and the need for God's unconditional love. There's a familiar hymn we sing in church that captures this sentiment—going to Jesus "just as I am, without one plea." This is precisely how we approach a loving God—without excuses, without deserving His love, and without hope based on our own merit. Yet, God promises to shower us with the grace love we desperately need.

. . .

IMAGINE if we showed this kind of love in our relationships. What if we loved our children and spouses unconditionally, regardless of their past, present, or future actions? How many families could be saved from turmoil and dissolution?

UNFORTUNATELY, it's all too common to adopt a conditional mindset, saying things like, "We'll work things out when she changes her behavior," or "He's flawed in these ways, so I can't fully love him." However, Jesus looks beyond our faults and failures and says, "I will love you despite everything." This kind of love perseveres through sickness, mood swings, stress, and life challenges. Grace love is about giving to those who don't deserve it.

WOULDN'T it be transformative if we embraced this grace love in our marriages? It requires looking past imperfections and choosing to love authentically, just as Christ loves us unconditionally. This kind of love has the power to heal wounds, mend brokenness, and build stronger, lasting relationships.

GRACE LOVE IS like a delightful seasoning that adds sweetness, favor, and goodwill to our interactions. Have you ever noticed how, when we're angry, every little flaw seems magnified? It's as if anger acts like a magnifying glass, making even the smallest imperfections glaringly apparent. We may interpret innocent actions as intentional provocations and jump to conclusions about others' intentions.

IN SUCH MOMENTS, we must learn to exercise grace love—to show kindness and favor even when our instincts urge us to react harshly. Colossians 4:6 advises us to season our speech with grace, akin to a chef adding the perfect blend of spices to enhance a dish's flavor. Just as a chef tastes food before serving it, we should consider the tone and content of our words before speaking, ensuring they carry the flavor of sweetness, favor, and goodwill.

GRACE LOVE BECOMES crucial when hurtful words seem warranted. It takes immense grace to respond with love instead of giving in to anger or resentment. I recall a time during my managerial role when an unjust decision was made to fire a cashier over minor mistakes. Despite my attempts to advocate for fairness, the decision stood, highlighting the importance of grace and fairness even in challenging situations.

IN MARRIAGES AND RELATIONSHIPS, the ability to season interactions with grace love is paramount. It's easy to love when everything is going well, but true love shines through when challenges arise. Love isn't just about meeting expectations; it's about extending kindness and favor even when it's not reciprocated. As we navigate relationships, let's remember the three dimensions of grace love outlined in 1 Corinthians 13:5 and strive to embody them even when it feels undeserved.

THE CONCEPT of grace love encompasses several key attributes that are vital for nurturing healthy relationships. One of these attributes, highlighted in 1 Corinthians 13:5, is that love "does not behave itself unseemly." This means that love is characterized by good manners and respectful conduct. It's a common experience for couples to display their best behavior during the courtship phase, only to reveal their less polished sides after marriage. This transition can be shocking for the spouse who suddenly witnesses behaviors they hadn't seen before, such as unexpected belching or other habits that were previously concealed.

· · ·

AN ILLUSTRATIVE EXAMPLE comes from preparations for the Beijing Olympics in China, where efforts are made to improve public behavior like spitting and loud belching to create a more favorable impression on visitors. Similarly, in our marriages, regardless of cultural norms or personal preferences, practicing good manners and showing deference to our loved ones' sensibilities contribute significantly to the success of our relationships.

ANOTHER ASPECT of grace love mentioned in verse five is that it is "not easily provoked." This implies that genuine love doesn't seek out reasons for anger or blow minor issues out of proportion. During the dating phase, individuals often exhibit remarkable patience and understanding, readily forgiving mistakes and maintaining a positive attitude. However, after marriage, these qualities can sometimes give way to impatience and unkindness. It's crucial to emulate the patience and forgiveness demonstrated by Jesus, who loves us unconditionally despite our shortcomings.

LASTLY, GRACE LOVE "THINKETH NO EVIL," meaning it refrains from harboring negative thoughts or assumptions about the other person. In disagreements, it's common for hurtful words or actions to linger in our minds, leading to negative interpretations and eventual conflict. Grace love, however, fosters a mindset of gratitude and appreciation, focusing on the good in the relationship rather than dwelling on perceived wrongs.

IN SUMMARY, practicing grace love involves maintaining good manners, avoiding unnecessary provocation, and refraining from negative thoughts or assumptions. By embodying these qualities, we can nurture stronger and more harmonious relationships in our marriages.

. . .

GRACE LOVE IS FUNDAMENTALLY BUILT on trust rather than threats. This concept is beautifully encapsulated in II Corinthians 5:14, where Paul describes how "the love of Christ constraineth us." Grace love acts as a powerful restraint, compelling us to respond to others with love and kindness even when they may not deserve it. This commitment to love unconditionally makes it challenging for relationships to spiral into constant conflicts because when you've already made the decision to love despite circumstances, disagreements lose their power to threaten the bond.

AN INSPIRING EXAMPLE of grace love in action comes from the story of David Wilkerson, as depicted in "The Cross and the Switchblade." Wilkerson encountered Nicky Cruz, a notorious gang leader in New York City. Despite Cruz's initial hostility and aggression, Wilkerson consistently expressed love and compassion, stating, "God loves you, and I love you, too." Even when faced with threats and violence, Wilkerson's unwavering love eventually touched Cruz's heart, leading to a transformative change in his life.

THE ESSENCE of grace love lies in its response to threats and challenges with implicit trust and affection. Contrary to the misconception that God is waiting to condemn us for our failures, grace love demonstrates God's boundless compassion and forgiveness. Just as Jesus showed mercy to the woman caught in adultery, grace love extends forgiveness and second chances even when deserved consequences loom.

IMAGINE the impact of grace love in marriages, where spouses choose to love despite imperfections and shortcomings. It's a love that refuses to resort to threats of bitterness, separation, or divorce, opting instead to say, "Despite everything, I choose to love you unconditionally." This kind of love fosters trust, security, and a deeper connection, making it a crucial element in nurturing healthy and lasting relationships.

THE TIMELESS MESSAGE of Jesus echoes through the ages, inviting each of us with open arms, saying, "Come unto me, all ye that labor and are heavy laden, and I will give you rest" (Matthew 11:28). Today, if you haven't yet encountered Jesus Christ, He beckons you to draw near. He longs to breathe new life into your soul, to grant you salvation and eternal life, regardless of how undeserving you may feel. His invitation extends beyond mere words; it's an offer of a restored relationship with Him, a promise of unwavering love that persists even if every other loved one were to forsake you. His grace love knows no bounds—it endures through every moment of your life, sustaining you through the lows and carrying you into eternity.

JESUS ISN'T WAITING for you to tidy up your life; He's waiting for you to reach out and receive His boundless love of grace. Today, you can invite Him into your heart and become a cherished member of His eternal family, destined for His heavenly abode. While your earthly healthy and fulfilling marriage home may remain elusive, the joy of an eternal home in Heaven alongside a loving God surpasses all earthly treasures.

EMBRACE the call to love with grace, following the example set by Jesus Himself. Let your love be marked by sweetness and favor, devoid of threats or ultimatums. Choose to love unconditionally, mirroring the love that Christ shows us each day despite our failings. In a world where love is often conditional, let your love be a beacon of grace and kindness, reflecting the transformative power of Christ's love in your life.

CONCLUSION

I trust you share my conviction for the potential of attaining a healthy and fulfilling marriage for you and your spouse. Although the journey may not be effortless, inexpensive, or swift, it offers immense rewards and excitement, surpassing any other life pursuit. Let's revisit the principles we've studied, which serve as the guiding instructions for building a healthy and fulfilling marriage.

FIRST, embracing **true forgiveness** empowers us to overcome our mistakes and distinguish between the offense and the offender.

SECOND, **choosing to love first** involves repairing strained relationships rather than waiting for the other person to start reconciliation.

THIRD, we explored the **self-sacrificial love** exemplified by Jesus Christ, recognizing the importance of offering ourselves unconditionally to our partner.

NEXT, we delved into the concept of **loving 'til death.** This means upholding our marriage vows of standing together through life's challenges and adversities and remaining committed to each other until the end of our lives, just as we promised in our wedding vows.

WE GAINED insights into the significance of words, belief, love, and the sacrificial nature of constructive **love, which uplifts and strengthens** rather than tearing down.

LAST, we explored **loving with grace,** which entails choosing to love regardless of what the other person may deserve.

THROUGHOUT OUR JOURNEY, we witnessed the unparalleled love of Christ, serving as a flawless model of what a harmonious home embodies. Beyond that, we marveled at the depth of love He extends to each of us. Despite any reasons we might conjure for Him to reject us, He continues to love us and invites us today to embrace Him as our personal Savior!

IF YOU PRAY to this loving God, acknowledging your sinful condition and seeking His grace and love through the death and resurrection of His Son, He promises in the Bible to embrace you as His own child! It's an amazing offer, one that would be unwise to overlook! To accept Jesus Christ as your personal savior, you need to confess your sins, believe in His sacrifice on the cross, and invite Him into your life. Since someone must pay for our mistakes, Jesus Christ offers to liberate you from the chains of sin and provide you with a fresh start in life! Begin your eternal relationship with Him today!

ALSO BY W. AUSTIN GARDNER

Are You Called? A Checklist to Discern Your Calling From God. Print Kindle Ebook

¿Eres Llamado Por Dios? Un Checklist Para Discernir Tu Llamado De Dios. Print Kindle Ebook

Austin Gardner is an author and speaker in both English and Spanish. He serves as the President of Alignment Ministries that helps support missionaries in Burkina Faso,Kenya, Northern Ireland, Peru, Ukraine and more.

World Evangelism Podcast

Austin trains young men and women for the ministry through the Society of Mentors in both English and Spanish

He has written Rising Above the Hurt as a free gift for you. You will find more as they are released on the website.

You are invited to read new article every day as well as the already published articles on Austin's blog by clicking here.

Check out Missionary Stories and much more on Austin's YouTube Channel.

Made in the USA
Columbia, SC
07 May 2024

35378355R00072